In Search of Thomas

by

Daniel V. Townsend, Jr

authorHOUSE®

AuthorHouse™
1663 Liberty Drive, Suite 200
Bloomington, IN 47403
www.authorhouse.com
Phone: 1-800-839-8640

First published by AuthorHouse   12/11/2008

ISBN: 978-1-4389-2423-6 (sc)
ISBN: 978-1-4389-2522-6 (hc)

Library of Congress Control Number: 2008910171

Printed in the United States of America
Bloomington, Indiana

This book is printed on acid-free paper.

This book is dedicated to my wife of sixteen years, Kathy Diane Moore Townsend of Lexington; and to each of my children Danny, Jenn, Mike and Rob. I am especially grateful to Daniel, III (Danny) who was in town and available to me in the trying, exasperating time or 6/28/05. This was a time I underwent surgery, which led to serious health difficulties. I dedicate this to my children and to my wife for the role each played at that time. Family is important to me. Children Jennifer, Michael and Robert are the reason that I am content in life.

Kathy Townsend

My 4 children Robert, Daniel III, Jennifer, Michael.

This work is a testament to look back and see how the Townsend family merged with many others in the past. They melded together what we feel and believe became our heritage. This search for Townsend identity has taken over one hundred and fifty years, and continues today with many in Eastern North Carolina still seeking, asking, and researching truth in this honorable quest. Needless to say the Townsend Association of American has been a constant resource throughout.

Contents

Chapter One 1

Chapter Two 29

Chapter Three.. 43

Chapter Four... 51

Chapter Five 69

Chapter Six 75

Chapter Seven 77

Chapter Eight 87

Chapter Nine 105

Chapter Ten 115

Chapter Eleven 129

Chapter Twelve 131

Chapter Thirteen 137

Chapter Fourteen.. 141

Chapter Fifteen 145

Chapter Sixteen 149

Chapter Seventeen 157

Chapter Eighteen.. 167

Chapter Nineteen *171*

Chapter Twenty *179*

Chapter Twenty-One *187*

ABOUT THE AUTHOR

The remarkable Daniel V. Townsend has had many facets of interest in his lifetime – in the sports arena in high school, in literary pursuits in college, and now he has embarked upon a quest to find his own identity by uncovering his lineage from Cumberland and Robeson counties in eastern North Carolina. In spite of professional and family responsibilities, he has managed to record his search for the Townsend descendants in an extraordinary and compelling step-by-step account, which has emerged into this book.

Mr. Townsend sees his mission not simply as genealogical but as a consuming search to learn more about the identity of Thomas Townsend, and patent patriarch of the entire Townsend clan and with whom he more clearly identifies. His research into his progenitors has been thousands of miles of travel, scores of personal interviews, hours upon hours of checking musty courthouse files and state archives to authenticate his search for those Townsend descendants who could shed light upon his family tree. His latest venture was a pilgrimage to Norwich, England, where Raynham Hall, one of the Townshend family seats, exists. He became affiliated with the Townsend Society of America, Inc located in Oyster Bay, New York, in 1982.

While yet a student under my tutorage during his senior high school years, I discerned early that deep within the springs of his nature, Dan Townsend possessed character traits and human qualities which set him high above other classmates.

This book, though largely biographical, is colored by perceptions and personal observations, which make what otherwise, would be laborious reading an intriguing insight into the life of its author.

Blanche D. Hodul,
Fayetteville High English Teacher, 1961

Blanche Hodul 1981

William Frank (L) & His Father William

PREFACE

This book is offered as a memorial to William Frank Townsend of Robeson County. Frank met an untimely stroke at age 53 and as a result of his departure from this earth; his family was thrown into great difficulties and never fully recovered.

The compilation of information contained herein was derived from an intensive search of the Townsend Family of Robeson County. The research began July of 1981 and continues to this date as disembarked for Norfolk, England, on a pilgrimage which will help me determine where our Thomas Townsend, born c. 1726, actually came from – who his parents were – and how we are all tied together.

INTRODUCTION

In the bitter winter of 1978 I was driving my company auto across the plains of Wyoming. The bone chilling cold and blowing snow made it a lonely drive between Cheyenne and Casper, about seven hours, depending on road conditions and the season. I kept thinking about my kin back in North Carolina seemed a million miles away and for all practical purposes, they were.

My immediate family had always been very close, and love was abundant among the Townsends with whom I had grown up. I missed them much and really wondered how or when I would ever see the front doors of my Carolina home again.

I recall that my family loved their life in Colorado. The vast, unused and sculpt mountain landscape of that place was breathtaking. In reality despite the view I had little time for life there. I only had time for work. I was only home on weekends, and spent most of that time working in the regional office, which was in my home.

I began to remember the prayer promises that are abundant in the New Testament, and I was struggling. We couldn't find a church that met our needs or gave us any satisfaction or peace of mind. My wife, a staunch Roman Catholic all her life, was even willing to go to a free church or a Protestant Church, but none was to be found that satisfied us or met our needs. The Catholic churches were too busy with business meetings and protocol to deal with religion; the "deep South" missionary churches were too full of emotional words and seemed out of place in the modern era Rockies. That "ole-fashion" religion or folk that were God fearing and family centered seemed to have vanished with newer version of the Church.

I began to believe that I had achieving my career goals, and my thoughts turned long-term towards my folks back in Carolina. So I prayed aloud as I rode through that bleak dark day in Wyoming.

I recall petitioning, "Please God, I believe we are not to beg, but to ask...but these are not my people, this is not my land, this is not my home...take me home."

The events that seemed to happen quickly after this day were hard to believe or even describe. The messages seemed to be loud and clear. There was a telephone call out of the blue from Tom Harris, President of Harris-Cuthrell, Inc. He and I had one time discussed my general interest in his firm in Rocky Mount, North Carolina. I had been living in New Jersey at that time. When he managed to find out that my New Jersey phone had been disconnected, he apparently called Hanes Corporation, my employer, and somehow found me in Colorado. I felt chills when I considered the timing of his call and the series of events that allowed me to fly back to Carolina on several occasions and see him.

Additionally, there was an experience when I was routinely flying from Salt Lake City to Boise. I sat beside a gent on a slow prop plane that day. I noted he was reading a Mormon Bible, I think, so I inquired. He was Baptist, but he was a lay speaker for the Christian Businessmen's' Bureau.

He told me a long and involved story about how his life in Los Angeles was dramatically changed. He told me how he had asked God, in Christ's name, to take control in his life and how hard it was for him to let that happen. He told me how long it took him to sell his L. A. home and complete a transition to the out-of-the-way land of Idaho. He didn't even plan, or want to go there, but…it didn't matter what he wanted. I learned a lot, and began to understand what might happen, or could be happening to me.

I took the job, Vice President of Sales, for Harris-Cuthrell, Inc. I still had not sold my Denver home, and certain spiritual leaders, namely one Dr. Baxter Maye Walker of Fayetteville, believes there is a clear-cut reason for this delay. He believes that I should work for myself. He said that I was not the type of man who thrives, long-term, working for others. He was correct, I believe.

Many things have happened since that bitter winter of 1978. I have grown a lot and learned a great deal. Regardless, many blessings have come forth. When I asked to "go home" I really didn't know what would be as involved Dad's parents died early and we had only one grandmother. I didn't know anything about the Townsends. One time I was with my Dad, D.V., and we talked about this. He said his half sister Mildred Townsend Powers was ill and in a rest home in Lumberton. We went to see her, and I asked her a lot about the Townsends.

She had an old cigar box of clippings and one was about William Franklin Townsend, my granddad, on the eve of his death. This started the ball rolling, and since then, I have written scores of letters, interviewed many people, visited the Archives in Raleigh, picked up the pieces to my family tree; and how we know who we are. I wrote County Norfolk, England and made a pilgrimage there in March of 1982.

It has occurred to me that our Lord often answers our prayers and needs in ways that we can't fully understand. It is very interesting and intriguing that before I could go "home" I would have to learn where it was…perhaps even what it meant.

My soul was searching, my dreams were not clear; yet many seemingly great things have occurred to me since then. More will develop, for I am not at peace, nor do I believe that all that needs to be done is now complete~

St Pauls Gathering

This brief description is of the Townsends of Saint Pauls, North Carolina. We are mostly concerned with Civil War era, our William Townsend of St. Pauls. His roots were deep within Robeson County. Back to Charles, Alfred, William and Thomas Towns(h)end, born Chowan County, NC in 1725.

William of St. Pauls was born on a warm spring day in Robeson County, April 22, in 1842. He grew up to become a tall man and walked upright with his shoulders held high. He grew the customary beard and stood almost six feet, six inches tall. He was a proper man and well respected in his day. He was a landowner, and he had strong ties to the South. He fought the Yankees in the North Carolina 19th Infantry and was shot in the upper lip while serving the Confederacy.

He, at one time, was a merchant on the Main Street in St. Pauls and had a general store on the site of Sugar's Men's Store today. He had farmland and had one wife, Orrie Prevatte, sometimes called *Ora*. She was from a good family of French origin. They both lived long lives. William died in 1927 at about age 86. Orrie lived on until November 2, 1928. She was 81 years old.

William Townsend was lean and loved to garden. He had a look of dignity about him, and his wife had lived with him at the *old home place*, about two miles directly west of downtown St. Pauls.

Ora's children apparently grew up healthy, and they were well known citizens of Eastern Robeson. They had gone to various churches as evidenced by the number of family members buried at different churches. The First Baptist Church was one of the ones they attended, as well as Back Swamp, Barker Ten Mile Baptist.

William led an honest, clean life. They said he was always busy working his farm and didn't use tobacco at all. Ora liked to eat later in life, and she savored the baking of her daughter in law, Inez Wells Townsend. She loved bread pudding as reported to me by Inez in 1982. Both William and Ora are buried in St. Pauls Cemetery off I-95, NC 20. This is the story of their reunion of 1982 and of the families that were issue from that union in Robeson County, North Carolina.

Chapter One

"Please God, Take Me Home"

My father was an orphaned by William Frank at age Twelve.
Growing up on a farm two miles from Saint Pauls, North
Carolina, D. V. was a happy boy who grew up not knowing
the luxuries of the modern era. Living at the old home place
of William and Orrie (Ora) Townsend, D. V. and his brothers
and sisters found life very demanding. Frequently the farm
required long days and hard hours that taxed the very heart
and soul of those living in the era shortly after 1920. His
father had lost his first wife, **Flora** Ausley with whom there

were two children, and ***Mamie*** Rich Carter Townsend was now gone, and ***Inez*** Wells Townsend had taken the mother's place with her own two children and father William Frank. It was a crowded home.

By age five, D. V. had lost his mother, a well-known lady from Vander, North Carolina. She was Mamie Carter Townsend, a tall lady who was the daughter of Big Dan Carter, who was 6'1" and almost three hundred pounds. She had grown up the eldest of Docia Carter in Vander. The Carters' well known throughout *eastern* Cumberland County.

When my grandmother, second-wife Mamie died of pneumonia, William Frank was left to take care of the children at the old home. This farmhouse allegedly near Parkton, had been in the Townsend family for decades. There were six children already

Mamie Carter

by two wives, and times were very hard as the Great Depression neared. Grandmother Ora were getting on in years, as was Grandpa William Townsend, and they could no longer not help Frank with the children.

With exception was the oral tales that *Civil War~ William* would tell Daniel Varser on his knee. Reportedly those were some memorable moments of young D.V 's life on the farm.

W. Frank, while visiting a friend in Pender County, met Ms. Inez Wells and subsequently took her for his third wife.

He removed her from Pender and brought her back home in Robeson, about 70 miles South. Inez was the eldest daughter in her family, and she was certainly the most eligible when Frank asked Inez to marry. These were times when a family couldn't survive without a woman. These were the tough times around 1926-28, prior to the Great Depression, which flattened the American economy and stole confidence and hope held by Southern farmers.

Inez came to the home and did her best to supervise the family of six, subsequently having two children of her own, Douglas and Claude. Frank, who was developing some bad health as a result of high blood pressure, continued to do all he could to keep the family together. Shortly after 1927 Grandpa William Townsend died, and his wife Ora and daughter-in-law Inez were left to carry household responsibility with the family. There was little food and very little money.

Frank had mortgaged the house in order to bring money in for them to live on. There were some farm property owned, but it brought in little revenue and these were hard times for these tough Townsend ancestors. *Inez recalls* trying to share what little there was with everyone. She spoke of a time when they had a slice of ham to split a half dozen ways or more. She wanted everyone to have something that was *good* even though it might not be much or even enough. Inez said that Grandma Townsend liked to eat and was fond of her bread pudding, which was apparently made out of leftover bread. Nothing was ever wasted or left to go bad.

Each day they would cook for that day. There was no cow when Inez came to the old home place, and they only had pumped water or black coffee to drink. Sometimes during the summer months, D. V. and his brother, Roscoe, would go to town on a horse and buggy and fetch ice. The town was two miles away. They would use this ice in the icebox but it did not last long. Most of the time when they had ice, it was used for iced tea. This was a real treat, though a rare one.

Inez remembers that William Frank or as she called him, William **Franklin**, was a good man in his own way. He was a loving man and had many friends. He was a pleasant person who smiled a lot. Many people remarked that in his life, Frank and his brother, Berta, looked so much alike that some people could not tell them apart.

As if the bad times and economy were not draining enough, the illness was about to visit the Townsend family in Saint Paul' s. One summer evening, Frank wanted to go down to the watermelon patch and he started out through the tobacco field. With him were his sons, D. V. and Roscoe. They were running along ahead barefooted in their overalls, and Frank followed behind *topping the tobacco plants* as he walked down furrows in his sandy loam fields.

D. V. turned to look for Frank, but he was nowhere to be seen. Frank had fallen. They heard him moan, "D. V., come." D. V. and Roscoe ran to his aid.

He was lying in a tobacco furrow with his head downward in the trench and he lay in a most uncomfortable position, agonizing. He was gnarling, writhing and pleaded with them to raise his head. He said, "***D. V., I think I have had a stroke. My head. Please lift my head.***" Neither D. V. nor Roscoe were strong enough to lift big Frank from the field. He lay baking in the sun until they were able to call neighbors to come and lift him on a tobacco sheet. There were no nearby Doctors or Clinics This was an era where people just suffered, in the heat summer, at home.

They carried Frank into the house where he soon lapsed into a coma. It was not long thereafter that Frank passed on, leaving the old home place in dire needs. Financially they were becoming desperate.

[Inez Wells pictured in center, between her two sons from W.F. Townsend, 1982. They are Douglas on left, and Claude on right side picture. Far left is D.V. Townsend (Mamie Carter); far right is John Townsend-Powers (Flora Ausley)

When William Frank died, Inez Wells-Townsend had nothing to keep her at the sprawling *old home place* with six children. She made the tough decision to return to her parents' home in Pender County. She had known Frank Townsend and his family for only five years. She had contributed much, had helped him in his garden, and had even worked the fields of the farm. A brave and strong lady, she needed to get along with her own life. Her home was Pender, her folks and family had saved it for her.

When the Robeson home was split up, so were Mamie Carter and William Frank's children. D. V. was sent eventually to Grandmother Docia Carter's house near Vander, North Carolina, in Cumberland County. D.V. was later moved to Winston-Salem where the Reverend Berta Townsend, his

Daddy's brother, lived. He grew up in the family of Carlyle, Ruth and Joyce Townsend, and his *new stepmother* was Lenora, whom he cherished. Carlyle was biter, selfish, and picked on D.V. as a boy. D.V. carried this negative boyhood bullying by Carlyle into adulthood.

The splitting up of the children was a traumatic experience. The lost parents were unbearable to the children. Painful psychological scars even into his adult psyche for D.V. the adult.

Brother Roscoe had blondish hair, blue eyes, and was most handsome. By age sixteen D. V.'s brother, Roscoe, had drowned in Bullard Mill Pond back in Cumberland County. He allegedly had had a heart problem, which may have contributed, to his death. It was the last day of school that first day of May. But, the water in the pond was still seasonally cold. His sudden death and additional loss to the crippled family added to the burden felt by D.V. Townsend and sister Beulah.

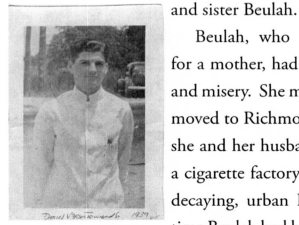

DV., *Army Medic*

Beulah, who had always longed for a mother, had a life of frustration and misery. She married too early and moved to Richmond, Virginia, where she and her husband, Bill, worked in a cigarette factory. Later she lived in decaying, urban Baltimore. By this time Beulah had health problems, and she was despondent. In 1973, the author went to Baltimore and returned Beulah to her Robeson County childhood roots. Living with Mildred Townsend-Powers near Lumberton, N.C. Beulah straightened her life out and became a reliable employee of Burlington Industries. During this time, she also secured an Associates of Arts Nursing diploma from Robeson Technical Institute. However, her old boyfriend later lured her back to Baltimore where she remained making baby booties until age and illness claimed her life in 2000.

D. V. sought a way out to carve out his own life. At age eighteen he enlisted in the U.S. Army. Shortly afterward he married Alma Sullivan in the city of Fayetteville, and a daughter was born. During World War II. As a part of being a medical corpsman from Fort Bragg, he was allowed to stay in the nearby city. In Fayetteville, he lived at the Sullivan Boarding House where he had met Alma Louise Sullivan. That became the first home for D.V. and Alma during the war years.

Following his military service, he ran Home Bakery and later worked at Mr. Sullivan's Boot and Shoe Repair at Fort Bragg. when Alma's father, Mr. J. A. Sullivan died. D. V. purchased the Sullivan Boot and Shoe Repair concession for Fort Bragg from his mother-in-law and followed the legacy of the *King of Shoemakers*, of the Sullivans. That title had followed the Irish Sullivan's from Burlington to Raleigh, to

Norfolk, and to two generations in Fayetteville. With the title came a proud heritage.

For many years, the Townsends prospered at 402 Pilot Avenue on *Haymont Hill* of Fayetteville. During these years, the Townsends became well known throughout the community for boot and shoe repair, leather care, and traditional shoe service in greater Cumberland County, N.C.

By 1950 they had opened Hay Street Shoe Shop as a second location of operations in downtown Fayetteville. Mother had managed and operated the store continuously until 2001. Mrs. Townsend was at the shop six days a week, taking few vacations. She was a business lady who loved working .She always wore a smile and loved the lord. She made the most of everyday so that she served her customers.

By the mid-1960's, D. V. decided to try several other business ventures in Fayetteville. He bought and began running the Happy Valley Meat Packing Company, the Fish House Restaurant on Gillespie Street, and the Shoe Trunk, a retail shoe establishment in Bordeaux Shopping Center. All of these ventures met with location, service and competition issues and led to D. V. Townsend's great despair. His family didn't seem worry, as did he, as he was personally involved with each investment. He grew more desperate.

Having financed himself to the maximum, D. V. became seriously ill and was hospitalized in December of 1975. At this point in time, he was near death. In time he recovered and enjoyed fourteen years of good health and prosperity. His family and Christian values had bided him well. Back in 1966 Dad wisely gave up control of the **Sullivan Boot and Shoe** Repair business at Fort Bragg. D.V. had spent almost twenty years signing government contracts. These contracts lacked a single price increase in all those decades. Now, D.V. and Alma began to concentrate efforts on a new outlet, Jeff's Shoe Shop on Raeford Road in Fayetteville. The two shoe repair businesses provided income for Alma and D. V. Townsend during their decline. Alma finally closed Jeff's Repair in Fayetteville in 2002.

The Townsends had four children. Mamie Patricia was the firstborn, in 1940, a bit of a tomboy but very popular. She was an average student and went on to become *Most Athletic* in her senior high class where she excelled in basketball. Electing not to go to college, Pat married Troy Jessup Allen. They had three children and resided on the old Clinton Highway near Vander. Today they live at Baywood Golf and Country estates in Eastern Fayetteville. After raising 3 children, Patricia elected to go back to college and in 1982-83 received her college degrees from Fayetteville State University. This has been a real milestone in her life and is a real plus for her career and a model for other women who had children early in marriage. Pat attended undergraduate

College with daughter Anita Allen who later became a California schoolteacher.

The second born child was James Daniel, who died of Sudden Infant Death Syndrome three months and seventeen days after he was born. So to say his was a Christmas baby and an Easter funeral child for mother and dad. This death was an incredible blow to Alma and D. V. and left a permanent mark on them. Many Christmases and Easters they make a pilgrimage to the Cross Creek Cemetery to put flowers on infant Jimmy's grave. Years of these visits served to haunt the living siblings. The children simply didn't understand the routine visits. They were never explained. One might think they felt a degree of guilt.

As a result of Jimmy's sudden death, the Townsends decided to have another child. It was the war years of 1943-44. This next child was Daniel Varser Townsend, Jr, me. I was a very happy and jovial infant but by the age of two developed serious respiratory illnesses. Following double pneumonia I developed chronic asthma and spent the next ten years in and out of hospitals

Most of biographical data is in the books *afterwards*. I should say that I shed most of the malady of early illness by age 12. Enjoying sports, academics and life in general I was a good student graduating from college and having worked regularly since age fourteen to twenty-one. I had various jobs: Laundry, Tobacco Warehouses, ASCS, Bowling Instructor,

Winn Dixie Grocery; plus I visited Mexico two summers. while still a High School student. Pictured on left side of page is Mary Ellen Dehmer in the mid sixties.

Mary D. Townsend

I had married Mary Ellyn Dehmer in Fayetteville. We had a planned wedding at St. Patrick's Catholic Church. It was very traditional, nice. I had several college fraternity brothers attend. One came from Gainesville Georgia, Gene Lawson, and Gerry F. Gill was from Laurinburg. Mary and I flew that day to Pennsylvania to begin our new lives in Amish country in Lancaster. The first year was a so much fun for us. Our income was great, our careers were terrific. Mary and I both worked and ate out most every night. I worked at Dewalt and she at Alcoa.

Then I was transferred as we began our family. We were relocated to Tarboro, North Carolina and proceeded with my career. We subsequently had four children between the years nineteen-seventy, and seventy-seven.

Mary is of German heritage and her family ties it seems are not nearly so close as my own. Her dad is a product of New York City, Notre Dame, and he was a devout Roman Catholic. Mary was born in Flushing, Queens New York on March 21, 1949. Her mother, also Catholic, grew up in South Bend, Indiana, where she met her husband Paul, while he was a student at Notre Dame. He was later a US Air Force Captain and in World War II combat. His Germanic story is striking as he was shot down over enemy lines and faced near death in flames as his aircraft crash-landed.

My brother, William Frank, came along on April 10, 1953 becoming the pride of our family. Frank suffered all the advantages of the modern era, and he was well taken care of and loved by everyone. He was a good student, popular, a nice looking chap who went on to excel in all athletics but especially in football. Like his brother and sister before him, Frank became the *Most Valuable Athlete in his senior class at Terry Sanford High in Fayetteville, NC*

Frank was awarded the full grant-in-aid to the University of North Carolina at Chapel Hill to play quarterback for Bill Dooley's Tar Heels. Following his graduation from the University of North Carolina's Business School, Frank was lured to Winston-Salem where Hanes Corporation employed the author. Frank enrolled in Wake Forest University's School of Business where he received a Master's Degree two years later.

Following this, He was recruited by Metropolitan Life Insurance in Boston, Massachusetts, where he remained for three years until he was able to negotiate a promotional transfer back to his hometown of Fayetteville, North Carolina. Frank married Jane Weeks, a Fayetteville native who had great musical talents and whose Fayetteville family had deep roots in the community. She was a bright individual who had graduated earlier from Salem College.

The grandchildren of William *Franklin* Townsend were of the middle class and began to make a name for themselves in the brave new world of the mid-1900s. Products of the nuclear age, William Frank's children were able to reach back and touch the land, with a keen eye on the future. The search for the Townsend identity has been an exciting one. It is the sincere hope of this author that the readers and their future progeny will use and benefit from this work.

Regarding the middle name Varser
An Interview with Mrs. Lilly Varser

One memorable day I had a telephone call from a lady by the name of Lilly Sneed Varser. During our discussion I learned that she was born September 29, 1911. She had called in response to my letter of inquiry requesting information on the Dutch name (my middle name) Vassar, or *Varser* as is it spelled in North Carolina.

She said that her father was a North Carolina Supreme Court Judge. His name was Judge Lycurgus Varser, Jr. He was a native of Suffolk, Virginia. His father, a pharmacist, was named William Henry Varser. His father had died of amoebic dysentery thirty days prior to her birth. He had been married to Emily Texas Duck Varser and they lived out in the County. Judge Varser lived with his mother until he was seven years old; then she died. An oil portrait of Judge Varser now hangs in the home of Lilly Sneed Varser in Lumberton. I took photos of that portrait and have copies for my dad, and son who share the name *Varser* with me.

Lilly Sneed Varser's address was 19th Street, at the corner of Chestnut. The greystone façade of the home features a brightly painted front door and street marker

Mrs. Lilly Sneed Varser told me that Judge Varser's middle name was Rayner. The name Varser is of **Dutch** *origin*. The Vassar family migrated to America with early waves of Settlers. The northern spelling was *Vassar* as in Vassar College in Poughkeepsie, New York. Those Yankees or one half the family that stayed north made their name in distilling alcohol, as well as through the college. The northerners that came south added a different spelling. They added an 'r' to the name. At least as a southern apologist, the county clerks spelled names as they sounded.

Judge *Lycurgus* (which means Roman law giver) attended Wake Forest College and graduated with an AB Degree in 1898. With graduation he was only twenty years old. By age twenty-one Governor A. W. McLean called him to join the prestigious McLean and McLean Law Firm in Lumberton, North Carolina. McLean was to become Governor of North Carolina in 1925.

Judge Varser was buried at Meadow brook Cemetery, but there is no vertical marker. The Location is in his Lumberton, NC. He is buried between Lilly Ford Sneed Varser and Heady Kate Aikin Varser. There is a bronze slab on the ground. This engraved monument celebrates L. Varser's life

To locate the grave near Biggs Shopping, one enters the front post of the cemetery. A person would then turn right and go toward three mature dogwoods in order to locate his gravesite. This is entering the graveyard from 24th Street with Old Fayetteville Road being on the right and Walnut Street being over to the left.

Lily S. Varser said she also had a daughter who went to Wake Forest and later completed her therapeutic training at the University of North Carolina. Mrs. Varser's daughter operated two clinics for therapy in Atlanta.

Judge Lycurgus Raynor Varser was born August 13, 1878, in Gates, North Carolina, just south of the Virginia line. He was an only child. He died October 5, 1959.

Basically, Varser only had two homes: Kinston, where he lived for four years, then Lumberton, where he worked and retired. He thought the world of Wake Forest and didn't seem to share this affinity for the University of North Carolina. The author realizes that many black and gold fellows have held bias against the Columbia blue and white of Chapel Hill, so I will print the quote understanding at Varser bore colors down to his bones like others before him and afterwards.

Interview with Mrs. Lillie Varser Benson,

East 19ᵗʰ Street, Lumberton, NC

Monday, July 19, 1982

Mrs. Lillie Varser Benson was about five feet, three inches tall. She was a lovely lady, and I do not know what her age would be. Her daughter was forty-four, so she could be sixty-eight years old or something like that. She weighed about 145 pounds and was rather stately. She seemed well educated. Her husband was a physician. The home was very nice, with room not terribly different in size as rooms in my original home at 402 Pilot in Fayetteville. The exterior was greystone and the rooms were decorated in very expensive furnishings.

It was a hot day; it must have been about 92 degrees. A note on Meadow brook Cemetery – Mrs. Benson lived right around the corner from Biggs Shopping Center. Biggs was a popular Shopping place at that time.

I never knew anything about the name *Varser* except that Judge Varser owned a farm next to William Frank, my grandfather. The Robeson Historical Society said that this was near Parkton, and that the deed existed in 1982 advised me. I also was told this story at the Townsend *reunion* on July 3 1982. Parkton Townsend's had suggested I visit the farm cite but I never did.

My father's name is Daniel *Varser* Townsend' Sr. His father was William Franklin Townsend of Saint Pauls. His marriage to Flora Ausley of Robeson ended with her premature death. His second wife was Mamie Rich Carter of Vander, near Fayetteville. This lady is my grandmother.

At that point he became close friends with neighbor Judge Varser. My Grandfather was a farmer and merchant in St. Pauls. His dry goods store was on the site of today's Sugar's Men's Shop. This retailer has been established for many years in St. Pauls the current era. Varser and William Frank hunted and fished together. Their farms grew vegetables for the table. My father, Daniel Varser, Sr. says that he remembers the name *Varser*. All my relatives say they remember Judge Varser. Folks remember seeing him at the Courthouse in Lumberton, NC.

William Franklin, my grandfather saw two wives die due to illness in the early 20th century, Flora Ausley was reported by The Robesonian as the "loveliest maiden in the whole of Robeson" on her wedding day as she departed St. Pauls for Richmond with Frank. Flora was mother of Mildred Townsend Powers. After her sudden death, Frank married again and wife Mamie Rich Carter was mother of Daniel Varser, Mamie Beulah and William Roscoe. The Townsend family was growing, as William and Ora were still living at the home place. After five or six years, Mamie was helping to slaughter hogs all night. This was a tradition when the weather was cold. Mamie contracted pneumonia, and died.

The 3rd wife, Inez Wells, would outlive Frank who had stroke at age fifty-three. She had two sons by Frank. Douglass favored Frank a great deal, and her youngest son was Claude. After Franks passing she returned to Pender County, in eastern North Carolina. That home is where I located Inez when I visited her for a taped interview with photos in 1981.

She explained that while she had remarried after returning home, that husband had passed also. We would do well to remember her story began about fifty years before. I was able to see her and talk to her about the reflections she had on years back in Robeson with the Townsends. I was especially intrigued with her two sons from that era, whom I met as a boy. She told me that Doug became a Chief of Police in Blowing Rock, the other, Claude stayed in Pender near his mother and Pender relatives. He married and settled there nearby.

My grandfather William Frank had died when my Dad, D.V. was going on twelve. His mother had been dead since he was about five years old. He was shipped off to Winston- Salem to live with a minister in the family, Reverend Berta Townsend. My father grew up in Winston-Salem, and the roots to Robeson County were lost until I began my search in 1980.

Mrs. Lillie Varser Benson told me that that her dad knew William Frank from farm life in Robeson. Her Daddy had a big farm out in Parkton. That was the same location. It may have been that connection that led to William Frank naming his first-born with Mamie, Daniel *Varser* Townsend on May 5, 1918. That lad was my father.

Back to the interview. During discussions Mrs. Lillie Varser Benson said of her father Judge Varser, "He was called Willie. That is why we placed on his tombstone, 'Willie Henry Varser'. He was married to Emily Texas. When the family migrated to America, the Northern spelling was 'Vassar'. Not that it matters, but you want to be accurate. They made their money in distillery. Those of us who came from the South were all Southern Baptists, and rather did not want to remember the Northern relatives, of whom we know nothing. We did not want to know that they were involved in whiskey production. Poughkeepsie is close to Albany. That is where Vassar College, N.Y. is located and our family has been removed since colonization.

Judge Varser's father was probably not the first to come south. I am sure it was farther back than that because he died thirty days before Daddy was born. Daddy was born in 1878 and lived until he was 81.

He was proud Wake Forest alumni, and the staunchest man. When he graduated, they did not have class rings or he couldn't afford one. He probably couldn't afford one. He graduated at age twenty with an AB Degree in Law. Reynolds Academy prepared him for college.

Reynolds Academy it was in Gates Co., Virginia. It is a private finishing academy that is also known as Reynoldson Academy. A person had to be twenty-one to take the Bar in North Carolina. At the age of twenty dad graduated Wake Forest Law School. He had to wait a year to take the North Carolina Law Bar exam. He had been away from law a full year and counted on farming because money was scarce. He also taught school during that year while waiting to take the Bar exam. Neither provided a good wage.

He came to Robeson County because he was in practice with Mr. Lofton in Kinston. I cannot give you his initials, but it was Lofton and Varser from 1902-1911.

In that time, Colonial (N. A.) Neal Archibald McLean died here. He was in practice with Angus Wilton McLean, which called the Law firm McLean and McLean. As I said, the first McLean died in Lumberton. And Angus called Daddy in 1911 from Kinston to move here.

They were acquainted when Daddy (Varser) had been down here and tried a case. Angus was impressed with him. They were very close to the same age. A. W. McLean was a few years older, maybe five years. Then McLean was governor in 1925-1929. Daddy wrote all of his legislative bills. Governor McLean felt a little insecure writing legislature, but Daddy had been in the Legislature in 1921 and 1923. He got the first North Carolina grant for building Pembroke State University in 1921. It was $75,000 and built the first building. So Daddy went to Raleigh and stayed a long time while the Legislature was in session, while McLean was Governor. Governor McLean was brilliant, but he was not comfortable wording statutes. So Daddy provided friendship and expertise which McLean needed in establishing laws of the state.

My father was indeed elected to the Legislature. He was a Senator in 1921 and 1923. In 1923, I was the first girl page in the world and earned money [like $2.00 a day]. I was thrilled silly. In 1925, (Dad) *Varser* was appointed to a vacancy on the Supreme Court bench. Well, we went there in the fall of 1925 and the life is very sedentary. Our family hated it, but most of all dad was bored. He said he wanted to get back in the courtroom and fight for his clients. He stayed less than a year, but it gave him great experience and he said he would not take anything for the experience in Raleigh working with McLean of Lumberton.

Then he became Chairman of the Board of Law Examiners. He was that for years and years. That is why I said he got the feeling---when you take the law exam you are given a number. Well, then they divide it up among the five members on the Board. So you check out and you grade just numbered pages. He said that he got so he could spot a lawyer from Chapel Hill. Their attitudes were slighted, and he vowed he could identify liberals. He said, "I could always tell a Wake Forest student. Their responses were brilliant." He was biased about Wake Forest law students.

Daddy was a Christian. Mother often told him that there was just enough money in teaching the Bible that he made the mistake of being a lawyer. He said that he had to be a lawyer to support *his little farm.* There is no way to survive a small farm unless you had a profession like Dad's. He grew tobacco, cotton, and before he died, soybeans. He too was close to Robeson soil, as he loved the farming lifestyle and the roots of Robesonian's.

There are a lot of *Townsends* in Lumberton. *Kate Biggs* was a genealogist of the Townsends, and she did research on the family. She died in 1972; she was a leader in Lumberton for decades. During the interview, Lilly went on to say,

"I knew Kate very well. She loved tracing family roots. She started much of the work that has been done."

I shared with Judge Varser's daughter, " there are other Townsends that are around that have also. I do not know them well. Walter Townsend, who runs the Sherwin Williams store, he and I are far related, fifth cousins once removed. He did come to our 1982 reunion."

Interviews with Immediate Townsend Family

Daniel Varser Townsend, Sr completed a resume for the book and it is below along with his comments.

Docia and Big Dan Carter's Home place

D.V.'s birthplace and his mother's home was in Vander, in Cumberland County, North Carolina.

NAME: Daniel V. Townsend, Sr.

BIRTHDATE: May 5, 1918

Photo of Grandmother Docia Carter, D.V.'s Grandmother

MARRIED: Alma Louise Sullivan (Jernigan) (Irish)

HEIGHT: 5'10"   WEIGHT: 170 lbs

JOBS: Quinn Funeral Home – Furniture Co
– Dunn, NC
Army – US Medical Department,
1936-1939
Owner and Operator of Home Bakery,
Fayetteville, NC
Ship Yard – Welding Dept,
Wilmington, NC
Owner-Manager, Sullivan Shoe Shops,
Fort Bragg (twenty-five years)
Watch Shop, Fort Bragg (two years),
sold to Purdy D. Faircloth
Hay Street Shoe Shop, opened 1950
– as of 1981, operated for thirty-two
years

Jeff Shoe Shop, Raeford Road - 1966-2001. Shoe Trunk Inc – 1969 – 1979 – family shoe store in Bordeaux, SC Sullivan Shoe Shops opened 1929 by James Alexander Sullivan till death in 1942. Carried on by D. V. and Alma Sullivan Townsend, sold in 1967.

HOBBIES: As a young man, liked to hunt, loved animals, sports, especially football and baseball

WHAT I REMEMBER MOST: D.V.'s comments below

Vague remembrance of Mother, Mamie Rich Carter. Age five, mother died, 1923 at age 32. Remember brother William Roscoe and sister Mamie Beulah, small, playing together. Remember going hunting with Dad William Frank. Going fishing and setting lines and overnight and checking them the next day. Seeing Granddad at age 86. Roscoe to tell neighbors William Sr. had passed away. Most hurt I remember was when my stepmother Inez came in my room. I had red measles and she told me my Dad had died. I was 12 years old (1932). William Roscoe and I had to go live with Uncle J. S. Townsend (Uncle Sandy) at Gray's Creek Township for about 1½ year. After then, I lived with Uncle Revered Berta Townsend and wife Lenora in Salem, North

Carolina approximately three years. Then I went to live with Uncle and Aunt Melie and Jane Lee – near grandmother's where Roscoe and Beulah lived about one mile away. By now, I was about 15-16. Worked with Melie and Mac Lee (son of Melie) at Quinn Funeral Home in Dunn, NC. From there to U.S. Army (1936). Met my future wife July 1937 while in charge of First Aid Medical Station – Courthouse in Fayetteville 1½ year. Next great shock was being notified that my brother William Roscoe had drowned in Bullard Mill Pond after school at the age of 16 on May 25, 1936.

I married Alma Sullivan. First child: Mamie Patricia. Pat was named for my mother (Mamie Rich Carter Townsend). Second child: James Daniel Townsend – born 1 hour 15 minutes after Christmas Day (on December 26, 1940). Crib Death Syndrome: passed away on April 12, 1941. (SIDS). This was one of the most devastating happenings in our lifetime. Third child: Daniel V. Townsend, Jr. Born on March 16, 1944. Alma and I almost lost him at six weeks. He was a very allergic child. Fourth child: William Frank. Born on April 10, 1953. Frank was a strong and healthy baby. Stood alone at 6½ months. He was our last child and we were felt blessed.

Alma said, "God blessed us in many ways. We still have three wonderful children and seven grandchildren as of this day, September 18, 1981, and one great-granddaughter, Patti Scott, who is Karen Allen's daughter."

Chapter Two

A Visit to Aunt Mildred T. Powers in Lumberton Mildred was D.V.'s ½ sister. Born to Frank and Flora Townsend. She and brother John were survivors from Flora.

It was a hot July day in 1979 when D. V. Townsend Senior asked his son, Dan, if he wanted to go to Lumberton to visit Mildred Townsend Powers, who was gravely ill.

D. V. said that she was one of the few members of the family who recalled anything in detail about the Townsend family. No one in D. V.'s family had ever really understood the Townsends or known much about them because they had been almost missing links since the passing of William Frank, D. V.'s father, back in 1930.

On this July day, Dan seized the opportunity to go see Mildred and was really surprised with his findings after he interviewed her. She had many recollections of both William Frank and Grandpa William and Grandma Ora of St. Pauls. She had saved many old newspaper clippings regarding early weddings and the passing of William Frank, plus other major events in the family history.

With this information being available, Dan began a long and arduous search for the Townsend identity. A trip was made to Winston-Salem to visit Joyce Faw in late July of 1981. During this trip, three Daniel V. Townsends actually stayed together at the Ramada Inn in Winston-Salem. Daniel, Jr. was attending a seminar during the day but D. V. and his grandson, Daniel III, spent a good deal of time visiting with kinfolk in Forsyth County. Little new information came from this trip but it continued to be a major goal to discover from whence they came.

Not too long after the Winston-Salem trip, Dan decided that he would make a trip to Lumberton. During this business trip, he stopped off at a paint store and accidentally met one Walter Townsend, the local manager. Walter related that someone in Lumberton had done extensive research on the Townsend line, but he was not sure how to reach the person. Later Dan was to learn that person was Kate Biggs who indeed had believed her findings proved the route all the way back to Daniel of Edisto Isle, SC and on to Boston, then England.

Several weeks later, Dan was in route to Fayetteville from Charlotte on business, and planned the trip to Red Springs, Robeson County. He first stopped at the most logical place, the Townsend Drug Store. Here he was disappointed to learn that old Mrs. Townsend, who had kept a lot of records, had passed away. Nevertheless, someone mentioned that there was a gentleman by the name of James Campen who ran an insurance office around the corner. Dan knocked on doors until he found Mr. Campen and interestingly enough, young James Campen, Jr. had just returned to Red Springs from Tennessee where he was a college professor. He had decided to move back to his home in search of the roots.

Jim escorted Dan down to talk with Alex Alexander, who was also of the Townsend line. He, an East Carolina graduate, suggested that Rebecca Wiley of Nashville, North Carolina would be the most appropriate person to help him. Jim indicated that he was going to go through his mother's old records and see if he could determine anything about Dan's line.

Following this suggestion, Dan did contact Rebecca Wiley of Nashville and the search continued. Rebecca referred Dan at last to some people who had extensive information. Dan wrote to Mabel Townsend of McDonald's and Mrs. John Townsend of Red Springs. Both ladies replied, but only Peggy or Mrs. John Townsend seem to have details he needed for his research.

Finally, one Daniel Earle Townsend responded and the search narrowed. Daniel Earle indicated that Peggy Townsend of Buie had written a book on the Townsend Heritage. Earl said that he had a copy and he was certain that Peggy would sell another one.

After several more weeks, he wrote Earle and received in the mail a copy of Peggy's book on the Townsends. Her pamphlet had been published in 1970 and clearly addressed the Townsend line, Dan's line. It was revelation for the Fayetteville family as continued study and research continued through correspondence, visits to libraries, and interviews.

D.V. was really elated and when Dan received the booklet. He and D. V. spent the better part of the next day searching the old gravesites at Gregory Cemetery (Lumberton Country Club) where William and Sarah Townsend were buried in about 1830. They continued over to Odom Cemetery where Dan was able to locate the gravesite of Charles Townsend. Charles's son Alfred (see picture) was to have been buried in this cemetery also, but since many of the markings were made of long-lasting lightwood, they perhaps had decayed. Charles' grave marking was etched in stone. All these names came from Peggy's research on Townsend's, which later were verified. I detailed a map of these gravesites and directions and placed in my original body of work, which was in non-circulation at Fayetteville Library, Ray Avenue, 28303.

After visiting these gravesites, D. V. and Dan made the trek to another location to see D.V.'s family, located the Townsend Family Plot and Central Cemetery about a mile north of St Paul's, Hgy. 301-S. following this, they went to Raft Swamp Baptist Church and Back Swamp Baptist Church to examine old tombstones of bygone eras.

It was truly exciting to be able to locate all the basic ancestors that were immediately related to dad and me. The chief problem remained: who was this *Thomas* Townsend, born 1726? How could they determine more about Thomas? Could Dan, through renewed energy and research, find out more?

At this point in time, Dan began a new quest, and contacted anybody and everybody associated with Thomas Townsend research. He was given the name of *Mrs. A. A. Ruffin* of Wilson. In searching for her, he found that she had moved to Miami, Florida. This Mrs. Ruffin, or as we shall call her, *Matilda*, had done extensive work on the family history for more than twenty years ago. A brilliant lady who was articulate *par excellence.*

Matilda Townsend Ruffin contributed many new ideas and Dan continued to gain a perspective on what needed to be done next.

Following extensive interviews with Matilda on her Christmas trip back to Wilson, Dan spent several hours in Raleigh at the Archives studying ancient records and searching for Thomas. Following this, Dan ventured down to Old Cross Creek Cemetery in Fayetteville and spent the afternoon searching for old markers in hope that somehow one of the graves of Thomas or one of his children might show up, but he found none. Even in the 1780 section of the graveyard, there were no clues.

This was in Cross-Creek, Fayetteville. Thomas' will was probated here, not in Robeson County formerly old Bladen County, North Carolina.

Next, Dan visited Peggy Townsend at her home, 35 miles south, in Buie. They continued to discuss alternatives and explore ideas and theories about discovering Thomas Townsend's roots.

Peggy had received some information from Microgen, a computer genealogical service from Salt Lake City. Dan recognized the importance of this contact and wrote for a computer listing of all those in their computer database who had sailed from England to America. This information was vague and sketchy and was not particularly useful. The Mormon Church as we later discover kept on developing files and research and today operates ancestry.com, an international database for family tree research.

Continuing the quest in 1981, Dan wrote numerous letters directly to England. He wrote to the City Counsel of Norwich and received a response from Mr. R. Banford, who was Director of Administration. Mr. Banford had undertaken to begin some research for him and referred Dan to the Townsends of Raynham.

Dan began to consider the possibility of visiting Norwich and Norfolk to conduct additional studies. He also wrote directly to Marques Townsend, who was supposedly still living in the Townsend Mansion in Raynham, near the village of Fakenham, not far from King's Lynn. No response was ever received from Raynham Hall's Marques Townshend. Daniel waited and waited, but post never came.

Dan continued his search and wrote directly to the Office of Public Records. He requested that they continue to send information to him, for a fee, regarding passengers and old records concerning those who sailed from England to America.

Several books were helpful in this research. *The Seven Townsend Brothers of Texas* by Tula Townsend Wyatt gave a perspective on the Townsend home of Raynham. *The Townsends of Old and New England.* This book was also a source of information and the publication gave pause. The last was about Thomas of Lynn, Massachusetts. These writings were enriching and gave me perspective and opened my thinking into the possibilities that are ahead in the research for our Thomas.

Correspondence received from Kansas post (U.S. Mail) indicated that there was a Thomas Townsend of Virginia who apparently migrated further west than Jamestown. Many believed the Thomas Townsend that Peggy and I know from research actually came down from James Citie, Virginia. Most of the Biggs research has focused on the 1688 Edisto Island-Charleston, South Carolina connection. Here information indicate that Daniel, who was the son of Thomas of Lynn, Massachusetts, did live and die on Edisto Island, near Charleston. Copies of the wills of Thomas, Daniel and William in the earliest colonial days of Charleston lead me to speculate that Thomas of Cumberland was related to Daniel of Edisto. Kate Biggs did believe this, before my time.

Peggy Townsend seemed to poke holes in Daniel of Edisto's date of birth, pointing out that he seemed too young to have fathered Thomas of Cumberland.

Thomas may also be illegitimate son of that line in Charleston, but regardless it was 1981 work in which I made this finding. Daniel Earle Townsend of Rock Hill/Blowing Rock, and son in Pleasantville, NY currently claim this line--- Thomas of Lynn. Both have access to DNA but none has been taken at this printing. This is 2008 data.

New information has continued to roll in and there are those today who believe there was a John or perhaps Nicholas Townsend Quakers and who relocated from Pennsylvania. Perhaps these are the true ancestors of Thomas of Cumberland.

Of course, there are perhaps some Townsends who landed throughout the eastern United States, such as Richard of Virginia in about 1621 and Thomas of Barbados in about 1726. There may have been Thomas Townsends in Charleston, South Carolina. Matilda reported this theory. She pointed out the search is precarious work. She believed that one would do well to determine where the settlement is of William of Charleston. If we determine the settlement, she believes we will be able to uncover who the sons were and where they lived. Perhaps this is the missing link for Thomas.

In early March 1981, Dan was able to make a business trip to Charleston area. Stealing a few quiet hours in the evening and in the early morning, he visited the South Carolina Historical Society in the "fireproof" building and located a genealogist to assist with the Townsend research work there. He has also located living descendents of Daniel of Charleston. Mr. and Mrs. Charles Townsend of Wadmalow Island apparently have extensive information regarding the Townsends. However, he was unable to secure information that proved valid or helpful in this quest.

One other possible source is Mrs. Harold Simmons, who was handicapped and unable to travel. An old acquaintance of Mrs. Fitzsimmons is Mrs. Simmons who had done extensive genealogical survey work for both Peggy Townsend and Matilda Townsend Ruffin years ago. Much of Mrs. Simmons' work was difficult to translate due to her penmanship, so Mrs. Fitzsimmons agreed to help decipher some of this work.

Additionally, Dan was in communication with Leland Townsend of Orange Park, Florida, who to published a book on the Townsends from 1066 to 1984. Leland's findings were confusing and Leland seemed to want Peggy and I tied to the Alexander Townsend line, of Red Springs. Peggy said that in his third attempt she kept looking for solutions, but they escaped her. Leland's controversial book was interesting for references, but seemingly inaccurate on at least one matter.

One other note, regards a genealogist in Raleigh who had done extensive research for Peggy Townsend some time ago. Apparently, this gentleman tried to tie Thomas Townsend of Cumberland to Andrew Townsend, who was the son of Andrew, the brother of Daniel in Charleston. Another theory is that Daniel had an illegitimate son, or unpublished son born about 1725 who was Thomas. This might be our Thomas, since Daniel was *about thirty years of age* upon arriving at Ediso Island. This theoretical line shows that we are therefore related to Thomas of Lynn, Massachusetts who was the first immigrant of that particular family.

It is noteworthy that Thomas of Lynn bore the Townsend Coat of Arms to the New World when he arrived here shortly after 1620. The coat was recorded in 1886 publication of *Official Baronage*, in London: Azure, a chevron ermine, between 3 escallops argent. The crest is a stag statant proper, attired and unguled. The motto---Hace Generi Incrementa fides.

The 1982 purpose of this manuscript was to provide an unabridged listing of all the information that has been discovered in the past hundred and fifty years as a result of the search for Thomas. By 2008, while the focus had expanded, concerns were the same.

Dan anticipated that the present residents of Raynham Hall in England might not receive him on his on his planned trip during the week of April 15, 1982. He previously sent them an audiocassette tape regarding the visionary purpose in making the pilgrimage. He also sent photographs of his family in an effort to appeal to their personal curiosity so that they might perhaps receive him.

Mrs. Ethel Townsend, who is a native of Norfolk, England and the Secretary of the Townsend Society of America, feels that there is a fair chance that they will receive Dan. Also, Martha Burke, genealogist for the Townsend Society of America, who at that time resided in Girardsville, Pennsylvania, believes that there is an outstanding possibility that Dan will be welcomed when he visits them. (Later, see her personal letter in selected letters chapter)

Whatever the case, we all know that these folks are somewhat beleaguered because out of the 10,000 or so Townsends in the world today, most all of them want to be tied to the Townshend Family of Raynham. These people are in the Royalty and they are listed in the official Baronage of England. They can be traced by to the Stamp Acts in Parliament during the Revolutionary War Period. They are Royals and thus titled, Marques and Marchioness. The conquering French made this Royal titular matter most honorable after Hastings, and a French Noble took the hand of a Saxon in East Anglia.

One story regarding the possible link to Raynham royalty. D. V. recalls that in 1928 his grandfather William told him " the first Townsend to leave England came to the Colonies to get away from his father. William went on to say to D.V. that

Mother, Alma Townsend of Fayetteville, N.C.

the elder English Townsend was responsible for the chopping off heads of those who broke the rules." That father was a powerful man, who had responsibility for passing judgment.

Some of the judgments involved beheadings." Perhaps this highly charged tale survived the years?

This unique family tale is a story that has been passed down. It is in fact

An oral history. Oral histories that have been passed down to many generations are noteworthy. Especially in light of the fact that the first *Viscount* of Raynham was a Townsend. The word Viscount in the English dictionary means *High Sheriff* and of course, a high sheriff of a county was responsible for passing judgment on criminals. The Viscount was named following England's Battle of Hastings (with the French) in 1066, and Anglia was home to Norman influenced Norfolk years later. Genealogists don't place much credulity in oral histories but Scots, and Americans void of record keeping seem to do so.

L

Chapter Three

Things I learned at the Knee of My Mother

I did not have your mother or just any mother. My mother was thoughtful, loving, and always teaching. She spent her days giving to her children. I remember many things about growing up. In 1999, Mother audio taped about two hours of conversation with me about her life. The following are some of my most vivid memories about my days with her at 402 Pilot Avenue in Haymont Hill, Fayetteville that was home.

Mother spoke candidly about accepting Jesus Christ as her personal Savior. She was at a tent meeting. At the tent meeting on the night she was "saved". She went forward in the service towards in Preacher during invitation. She was with girl friends that joined her at the front of the tent.

Afterwards, the girls sang Christian songs all the way home, dancing along the railroad tracks off Russell Street.

That night, Alma L. Sullivan quietly fell to her knees as she prayed. Her faith throughout her life gave me as a child and later young adult, confidence a plan to do the same. Follow the same plan as she had done. I also recall her mother reading the bible each day. Wow, what strength they gave me in this private area of my character.

THE CRIPPLING EFFECT OF DISPAIR

I appreciated the story of just how athletic Alma had become while swimming every Tuesday at the YMCA. The Pool was very convenient to her home and she was a regular.

She was accomplished as a High School Tennis player. It seems that my father had entered her life for this story. She and dad had had a spat and with this dejection in mind she faced the citywide play-offs with little or no support. It seems that Peggy Averitte, her opponent had coaxed a few friends to be quite verbal during their match.

This was an annual Central High Championship. Peggy arrived with a group of her friends shouting and questioning each call of the referee. Ultimately, Alma lost the match and dejection ran deep in her psyche. Her self learned motto after that was *be ready when the opportunity is there*, or the chance will pass one by!

The Disobedient Child

One-day mother had chased me through the house at 402 Pilot Avenue. She was after me for misbehaving. I had jumped chairs, leaped over small tables and begged her not to hit me. As I gained the lead, I sprinted into the kitchen and darted under the table. Eventually, Alma returned to the kitchen, washing soapy dishes and began singing. When I was about to sneak out unnoticed, she filled up a hot soapy glass with dishwater and threw it under the table dousing me completely. I was startled! Mother knew I had been hiding under the table all along.

YOUNG LOVE

When is love too young to last? I ask the reader this question because Mother said, she had married too young.

During World War II Charles P. Carter, D.V.'s uncle loaned his car to Alma and D.V. who eloped to Dillon, South Carolina. That was a popular state and town that did not require a birth certificate or parental permission for a couple to wed. My parents weren't the first is our community to use this resource. She cited Vivian and Herman Bishop as well as Vincent and Mrs. Shields who did the same. Reader I must tell you that these marriages were lifetime commitments all three of them.

Prior to marriage, Alma declares that she was not generally interested in boy **per se**; however, when D.V. a handsome young Army medic began rooming at her mother's boarding house she noticed him immediately. She was just over fourteen years old when she met Dad. Alma regrets not having waiting nor having time to grow up and learn more about life. She doesn't regret any of her four children after her marriage. Nevertheless she counsels, *if you can stay single as long as you can, even if you must bite your lip.*

How to teach siblings to quit fighting.

Alma had seen her children, Pat and me, nip and pick each day. We knew where each other's *hot buttons* were. We pushed them every day. One spring day when Pat was about twelve and I was about four years younger, we began the fight of the century. Beginning in the bedroom, we moved to the hall and on to the living room. Mother had had enough, simply locked the door from the outside and took a lounge seat in the backyard. Neighborhood kids were peering in windows as Pat and I proceeded to scream, kick, hit, and cuss. We slammed, punched, and struggled for hours and the neighbors thought Mother was insane to let us carry on for over and hour. At the end neither of us could move a muscle. The house was a disaster, but Pat and I never fought again. Plus, we had clean up detail for a month. Alma's solution worked.

The Nature of Work and its Reward

I leaned about work through my mother. She worked for over thirty-five years running Hay Street Shoe Repair. Dad had invested in the downtown Fayetteville business and before that, her father J.H. Sullivan had such enterprises in downtown for sixty years.

Mother would work six days a week, and after church she would return to she shop to scrub the floors and clean the shop. It was her meager income that proved the $35.00 per week that she sent to me during my four years at Wake Forest. Alma taught me that nothing was accumulated over night. While at Fayetteville High, I recall having one pair of pants. I didn't think *I was without,* but the value system that we grew up taught us that a dollar was something to be saved, not wasted. Mother didn't waste. These were the fifties, and sixties a time when many prospered, but a few still had values. Hard work was a good value.

Mother taught herself how to remember important things

I learned that while most men forget where they put their shoes or car keys, or an anniversary, women like my mother, were so special when it came to vital remembering.

When telling me of J.H. Sullivan's Wild West train show, she spoke of his *Oklahoma Days.* These were the days when the side of his rail car would drop down and become a sideshow. Much like the medicine shows of folklore or wagons,

Mr. Sullivan would peddle his wares and his trains made its way back to Carolina. On one particular trip he married an Indian girl from Oklahoma and brought back to finally set up a home. Only mother could say her full name. It was,

Lucy Virginia Hepsey Catherine Liza

Jones Summers~Sullivan.

Mother could just remember names, dates and important things like that.

A morning smile, a constant smile

When at 402 Pilot Avenue I always saw mother laugh and smile. She began each day that way. I began believing that life must be a good thing and that we each should learn to smile.

The storyteller's legacy

Mother said that *Lucy Virginia* was so loved that her mother, Viola, continued her spirit by naming her first child, *Virginia* .on December 20, 1916. Wonderfully that lady, my aunt, enjoyed a very long life span and is the centerpiece for the Wilson family in Robeson.

In turn, that Virgina saw the name further perpetuated in her granddaughter *Ginny*. Her Daughter Mary Louise had seen to it that *the girl from Oklahoma* had a long lasting trail in Carolina.

Mother had the knack of telling stories that begin six generations ago about the Indian squaw who joined the Sullivan family, and how she has a namesake alive today.

Mother's Comments

I don't think we understand how much we retain family ties and characteristics. One day, Mother told me, *you are so much like my brother James*. As always, I said, *I know*. But the truth was I didn't know. She simply had told me that for years. She also would say, *Coble D. your first cousin is so much like my brother Harry*. I never knew how to respond to mother's analysis. James was a sales type, and Harry was much more relaxed, laid back. These family traits did not seem important to me at the time, but today I recognize them as very true. Mother was always right.

Mother's last year on earth

My dear dad had died of pneumonia following a stroke back in September 2001. That month and year will be remembered for New York twin towers, but I remember if for <u>my father</u>.

Two years later, Mother had congestive heart failure. I didn't want to face her demise. She slept quite a bit, sometimes nineteen hours a day. She ate very little. She spoke to me one day saying, *I don't want to die Danny*. I took that somber feeling and look on her face to realize how each human ultimately feels at the end. Her wits were in tact and she simply wasn't ready to quit. Christian heavens seem a long way off at times, but she would always pull herself together and say *well, no regrets, I have no regrets son*.

Chapter Four

Copious Notes from Matilda Townsend-Ruffin

Today is December 18th, 1981. Leaving my home in Rocky Mount, North Carolina, we have a cool, winter day. It is snowing, mixed with rain. The roads are covered with a coating of ice. I drove down to Wilson, North Carolina from Rocky Mount heading down Highway 301 South to interview Matilda Townsend Ruffin. Matilda is a native of North Carolina (She has since finished her life in Miami passed on the hereafter, and her brother and Daniel Earle Townsend of Greenville, South Carolina have copied her research work.)

Through research letters, I located Matilda and she agreed to speak with me regarding her research into the Townsend Family Tree. She had done much research, perhaps as much as Peggy Townsend. So I was hopeful I could gain some insight into where I needed to focus my search in order to ascertain where Thomas Townsend was born in 1726, and in what setting; who his father was; and where Thomas is buried. Of course, many researchers are still wish to find the English Old Country link to our Thomas Townsend.

Mrs. Ruffin: *"In my Mississippi records, there was an early William Townsend who was before all the other Townsends in*

Mississippi. I think he was the brother of this Thomas Jr. He stayed in North Carolina, and his son sold his land.

Thomas Townsend Jr. was the son of Thomas Townsend. Our Thomas Townsend had sons in North Carolina. They inherited his land and sold his land. Every last one of them then went to Mississippi. All five of them went. I have proof of them in Greenville, Mississippi.

I made my Mississippi connection after a couple of years of trial and error. I knew that my great-grandfather had two brothers who went to Mississippi in 1839. There was an older Daniel Townsend and William Townsend who were in Mississippi even before these two men. I have never traced them; however, I am of the opinion that the Thomas Townsend who went to Cumberland County had two sons named Thomas and William. Thomas, Jr. stayed in Robeson County. He inherited the land. William inherited chattels, i.e. beds and horses. I believe William went to Mississippi. I believe the other one who stayed in Robeson County is our ancestor. This is where I have been stopped in my research findings.

I don't think there are any or very few at all of Charles Townsend descendants in Asbury Cemetery, because that line is the Alexander line that was Charles' brother. So all the descendants there are from "Alexander Townsend."

Matilda mentioned several interesting facts or rather beliefs. First, she believed that Thomas Townsend might not be our man. She espoused the theory that William and

Sarah (Thompson) Townsend might be linked to a William Sr. instead of our Thomas.

She continued, *there was a Thomas, and he had sons William, Thomas Jr., etc. We know that he married Letisha (Lettice) McConkey, that he died and left a will in Cumberland, leaving land, etc. to his sons in Robeson County.*

Interestingly, Matilda also highlights that David Townsend's work in "Harlee's Kinfolk" mentioned that William of Robeson's father was "William." This work was done in the post depression 1930's as a part of the New Deal. The research in "Kinfolk" was sponsored by U.S. government funds in F.D.R. 's New Deal legislation.

Another comment she made concerned Letisha's father Alexander McConkey. She noted that one Alexander McConkey appears in New England and at a New England 'experimental township' constructed near today's Georgetown, South Carolina. No other place has she found two Alexander McConkeys.

She believed that that name and family died out in Bladen County, North Carolina. Bladen was the stopping off place for the Scots in 1747, after most navigated up Cape Feare River. Georgetown, on the other hand was 110 miles south.

Matilda believed that the early work done by the late Kate Biggs in Lumberton several decades past was incorrect. Allegedly, Mrs. Biggs traced the Townsend line back to New

England vis-à-vis Daniel of Charleston, South Carolina. Matilda noted the birth date of Daniel as recorded in the Townshends of Old and New England clearly showed Daniel was too young to have fathered the lineage as depicted by Mrs. Biggs' writings. You will find Biggs's work in the public library, perhaps still in boxes.

After her death, her son was later the mayor in Lumberton, North Carolina, but he never ordered the work organized. Publically Mrs. Biggs supposedly refused to answer Matilda's letters questioning the birth dates of Daniel. In addition, Mrs. Biggs was to have said she would burn all her work before she died. Her work and research, though perhaps self-serving, inspired others to study genealogical documents thereafter.

Matilda mused, *that I had took her out, or rather forced her out of retirement.* She expressed interest in my continuing to develop new ideas and find facts. One theory is that a Scottish connection may exist. I believed that McConkey probably came up the Cape Fear River along with all the other Scots, after the battle of Ulster and the Spanish Alarm of 1948. It is plausible that Thomas either came with the Highlanders, was one of them, or met Lettice (his mother-in-law's name for his wife-to-be) when they came up river.

Matilda Townsend Ruffin and Peggy Townsend both point out that the Pee Dee River has a northern branch that splinters into Robeson County from near Georgetown, South Carolina. Perhaps this was the inland route of our Thomas.

Another idea is simple. He may have been a descendant of the Richard Townsend family, from near James City, Virginia. We know that the Albemarle precinct of North Carolina opened to settlers about 1700. Also, we find a Captain Robert Townsend and a William Townsend in Carolina precincts near the timetable we are seeking. We later find a Joshua Townsend in the Warren-Halifax area during the 1776 Revolution and the years afterwards.

There was a steady stream of settlers moving southward from Albemarle into Nash and Wilson Counties. With Thomas's birth date fixed c. 1726 I believed he existed concurrently with other Townsends from Albemarle; hence, he may be of that line. If so, we have a *bona fide* English lineage, genealogy, but not a Scottish connection.

Our search of land plats and early colonial records do not seem to help much because so much has been lost in fires. Matilda's work showed our family line i.e. Thomas, Jr. to Mississippi. She is familiar with other Townsend branches also. Her index of materials was obtuse, but full of data.

Matilda said, "Thomas' last will exists. The City of Fayetteville has the copy on micro file, but they may have sent the original to Archives in Raleigh. You should just ask them for a copy. They may be able to locate a settlement of the will. I have never seen a 'settlement' of Thomas Townsend's will. He died in Cumberland County in 1796. I have never seen the original will but I do have a copy of it. It is available on line. The will was probated on a July; at least that is when his daughter, Letisha (Lettice) signed the copy that Peggy sent me. Lucretia was the name of his daughter. His wife's name was Letisha. Her mother was Mary Maxfield. It is a shame that we are stuck.

When you go to England, it is much easier if you know who the immigrants were, whom your original ancestors were. It is unlikely that the South Carolina Light Townsend line is our family line. There was a book published years ago by a lady in Texas, named Mrs. Valentine. I did not get the book at that time. I had corresponded with her. I don't know if that was the **Seven Brothers From Texas** *book. It may have been called Seven Brothers. I have seen the Tula Townsend book. Peggy has that copy of the book.*

Let's talk about Irish Ulster Plantation home of many colonial emigrants to our land, and particularly Bladen County later called Robeson.

Ulster County is in Northern Ireland. It was awarded to English Nobility to settle in Ireland. They were given land grants. And they took Ulster County away from the Irish and pushed the Irish out. **Stir of the Irish Race** *is an interesting book in which the Irish give their opinions of the relocation from Ulster. Some Scotch people were put on that plantation and some English went there.*

I added, "Many Irishmen including our Matriarch Sullivan who married English Royalty, e.g. Lady Tuttonton came to America 1850 and thus become part of Carolina's melting pot heritage." That is my mother's family-line.

Matilda continued, *Johnson was Governor of North Carolina at the time of the Battle of Culloden. That was in Scotland and Scots lost the heads of their clans. Clan "tribes" no longer had their historical family power. North Carolina's Governor Johnson, who was Scotch, recruited settlers from Scotland and many of them came from Ulster Plantation in Ireland. Emigrants came up through Cape Fear River and tributaries. Fewer of them went up into the Piedmont region of the state up tributaries like the Deep River. This was the second factor in immigration that affected the Cape Feare Basin in Thomas's era. Some of Scots settled up around Fayetteville and Robeson County. This was right before the American Revolution.*

The reason that they did not fight as Tories was because after the battle of Culloden they had sworn that they would never raise their hand against the King of England again. They felt obligated enough so that they would not fight on the side of the Colonial, Carolina Patriots.

I am not sure if Horatio was the first Viscount in England. Sir Roger of England was the father of Thomas of Lynn. Horatio was the oldest son of Sir Roger. At the point of Sir Roger is the point where our lives become collateral with Thomas of Lynn. The oldest son was the beginning of the line that advances to the contemporary era of Lord Marquis Townshend and Raynham Townsend.

Some Townsends of Mississippi are looking for a connection to Raynham. Some are vaguely a relative to us or perhaps not at all. Some have been able to help several people, like Solomon Townsend. was an acquaintance of Thomas. He was one of the Townsends of the Spanish Alarm near Wilmington in 1747.

Solomon is completely separate from Thomas. I have enough records on him to show that he is separate. There are records about the children from Solomon Townsend and Thomas Townsend, land grants, and migration trails.

The Townsend's in Mississippi say that one of the problems that they have had was that in the early years, the 1800's, the people that came there, came young and were uneducated. They brought up their children in the wilderness frontier, and unless their mothers could teach the children, they did not become literate like their family back east. So they had to start all over again. Thus, they did not have many records.

Regarding Thomas of Cumberland County he remarried. Apparently Leticia (Lettice) McConkey Townsend had died, and his sons were administrators of his Cumberland Co will as well as Willis a Negro or mulatto family member. He had purchased 100 acres of land near sandy creek, near today's Grannis Airport-Field in Fayetteville. Thomas his children signed as administrators. His daughter did. So evidently his wife was dead. In the Census of 1796, Thomas Sr. shows up with about four women in the household. They were his daughters who were not married. He had sons over in Robeson. They were forty-plus years old. William was born in 1750. Thomas, Jr. was born in 1764; that is fourteen years. Now he is up in Cumberland in 1790 and his children did not get married until 1802 and 1803. This is not likely. They could have been adopted, and he may have married another woman. But she wasn't listed on his will. He does not even mention a wife in that will. He doesn't mention Thomas or William; nor does he mention a wife. He has children that are not even married. So they were not old maids. There is such a gap of information with this will.

Now I do not know when Letisha McConkey died. Mary Maxfield married again after Alexander McConkey died. She married again apparently after Alexander.

I don't think McConkey was in Robeson or Cumberland. I have one or two items on McConkey. There was a Ruth McConkey; there was a Robert McConkey. Robert McConkey is the only one I have in Bladen County deeds. Of course, Alexander died in Bladen County and so did his brother, Patrick.

The estate of Alexander McConkey was settled by inventory by Jean McConkey. The clerk of the court wrote it Jayne McConkey. But she signed it in her own hand 'Jean'. She was Scotch and she pronounced it 'Jane.' So he wrote it 'Jane' because the tendency of country folk to write things the way they sounded.

I have no idea who Jean McConkey was. She may have been his daughter. I don't know. Robert McConkey is mentioned in Mary Maxfield's will. There are Mississippi Townsends who have used the name 'McConkey' in their names.

One of Alexander Townsend's sons, who were named Alexander, went to Mississippi. At the same time Thomas Townsend Jr's sons went to Mississippi and he was also named Alexander. They settled in the same part of the state and one of them became Alexander McConkey, that is Thomas Townsend Jr's son, but our Alexander, who was a brother to Jackson, my great-grandfather, called himself Alexander Franklin.

Matilda went on to say "it was her opinion that neither Townsends' had a middle name when they went to Mississippi They adopted a middle name so that people would not get the two of them mixed up. Up until the middle of the 1800s, it was most unlikely that any Townsend have more than two names, just a first name and his last name. Therefore, more likely they did not use a middle name. It was only after the middle of the 1800's that you find more than two names.

There was another Townsend. This Townsend was the father of this William in South Carolina. His father-in-law's name was Steve Boden. Steven Boden was the father of Sarah Boden, who married this William. She was the mother of his first five children. These first five children are mentioned in Steve's will. This will is very important because it confirms the same children that are in William's, the father's, will. This name "William" was established and the first wife's name was "Sarah". She was William's wife. And his second wife's name was 'Thormozon" and she bore him two children.

This is the William Townsend who was born in South

Carolina. He disappeared and they called him "William of North Carolina." He was called this in either William's will or Steven Boden's will. But in one or the other.... I think it is in William's will or Steven Boden's will, which was the grandfather of this boy, also called all the children by name except the last two children by Thormozon. It confirms which set of children was which.

McConkey and Thomas, Sr. were Quakers. You will find that in Grind's Wills. There are two volumes of Grind's Wills and among these Carver's Creek things, that McConkey was involved in a lot of many different will, as executor and witness. Thomas Townsend, himself, was in one or two of them."

I was recalling when it was that I first learned of the existence of Matilda. I believe it was her sister, Miss Mabel Townsend of McCall in Robeson County who mentioned her in letter, but it might well have been Peggy Townsend in Red Springs. It has now been almost a year since I began to search for my roots and for Thomas' origin in Carolina or Virginia.

I learned that Matilda lived in Miami but returned to Wilson, NC to see her mother periodically. I asked if she would grant me an audience, and she did, around Christmas time in 1981. I was ecstatic at the prospect of meeting another Townsend descendant who had done extensive research on the origin of Thomas Townsend.

Matilda was vivacious and full of herself. She spoke with an uncanny spirit and command of the southern aristocratic English. She had phrases and words that told me that she was special. Matilda listened impatiently as I tried to tell it all in a few moments. I now believe she was bored or didn't care. She must have respected me by allowing me to speak, or rather ramble on for a while.

Soon, she began to pour out the details of her knowledge bank. She spoke of history as if she were actually there. She gave glaring accounts of the use of rivers for early Americans. She spoke of the Alford's, the Thompson's, on their migration from Virginia into Northeastern Carolina i.e. Nash, Edgecombe, Wilson and down East Counties. She painted a clear portrait of her genealogical work. Her mind was clearer than any I had ever encountered. Her lucidity was provocative. I chose to accept her as genuine, and though our styles and personalities differed, I appreciated her quest for excellence. I even believed that her motives are purposeful.

However, I never sensed that she really cared to "finish the task". She seemed perfectly content to recap again and again all that she had learned. Her stories would fill untold pages!

She did come to my Rocky Mount, North Carolina home for dinner shortly after our first meeting, and my children and wife shall never forget her visit. She talked faster than most could hear. Matilda speaking was like a machine gun firing. She wore my family out, but not me. I continued to marvel at her zest and fervor. She was indeed, full of herself, to the point of exasperation.

I wanted the cassette tapes that I had recorded during her visit transcribed and entered into the permanent treatise on *In Search of Thomas*, but she objected once I sent her the first transcript. Matilda was deeply sensitive, and a novice like myself learned to take care not to ruffle her. I learned this the hard way and received some biting letters from her. She scolded me time and time again about her take on my hurried approach to seeking data on Thomas Townsend. My vantage seemed simple. I had a fulltime career, and Thomas Townsend had to be attended to as best he could, when I can find or steal time from my regular vocation in Sales Management.

Matilda Townsend Ruffin was seemingly one of the keys to my research, and the future of my quest and search for Thomas. She had a special quality, a salient confidence that was evident upon meeting her. I chose to believe that she contributed to the finding of our Thomas. God willing, I will follow up on all her ideas and suggestions. I want to find the missing link. We are probably closer than some think.

Research Notes from Matilda's Data:

Gen. #1. - Richard Townsend of Va. (in early 1630's, burgess, etc. James City)

Gen. #2. - Robert

Gen. #3. *– William (Note this man)***

Gen. #4. - Joshua, b. aboutl735- died 1772. Inventory in Northumberland Co.J Gen. #5. - Ewell Light

Gen. #5. – John Died (Boonesboro, Ky.) Notes from Tula Townsend Wyatt Oswald Thomas R. (to Fayette, Texas) Asa Spencer

Joshua, Gen. #4, above had a brother named William. William married Elizabeth Haynie. They had two sons, Haynie b. 1745 and Griffin. In the "Oblong" section of New York State, Noah Townsend had a son Joshua. No dates.

JOSHUA TOWNSEND OF N.C. In the 1769 Tax list of Dobbs Co., N.C., and JOSHUA Townsend is listed as "1 white poll". This list shows only slaves and white men over 21. It does not show women or children, so it proves that he was there and taxable. * Dobbs County has disappeared into Wayne Co., Lenoir Co. and Johnson Co. N.C (MTR* notes for Daniel T.)

From the ROSTER OF SOLDIERS FROM N.C. IN THE AMERICAN REVOLUTION, by DAR Page 194"Joshua Towson Page 394"Joshua Tousan- Hillsborough District. Page 99 "1780-82" Page 50 "1780-82" Page 231 "Joshua Tousan -#50- Vol X- Folio, page 3 Page 601 - Joshua Tucson, reed his bounty of the aid volunteers & Drafts from Wilkes Co. (N.C.) 1-19-1779.

Page 278 land grant to heirs of Joshua Thompson---acres to

John Price 1783,10 (I think further research will show this is Townsend not 14 Thompson) 1796-Will of Thomas Townsend of Cumberland Co., N.C. delegate-Son: Joshua

HATHAWAY states "1827 "Will of Joshua Townsend: Names Sons, John. P. Townsen, Joseph W. Townsend and Calvin I. Townsend." **this is a mistake in Hathaway-: The three sons, John P. Townsend, Joseph W. Townsend and Calvin I. Townsend were-the sons of JOSIAH TOWNSEND who died in 1827. (Perquimans Co., N.C. Townsends who migrated west toward Guilford Co., N.C.)

1. Land grants Richard T. of Va.,
2. Battle of Culloden
   "Official Heritage of England"
   Descent of Thomas. T. Of Lynn, Mass.
   1790 Census of Cumberland Co., N.C.- Thomas T.
3. Thomas of Cumberland Co. and Thomas and William of Robeson
4. Thomas and Wm. of Robeson
   Two Thomas T.'s of S.C.

5. Thomas #1 of S.C.
6. Thomas # 2 of S.C.
   Thomas of Lynn, Mass.
   Daniel T.'s grandfather in 1630
7. To do research in Charleston
8. Solomon T. (Anson Co.) of N.C. & S.C.
   Quaker records of Carver's Creek & Cross Creek—N.C.

9. Quakers Of Eastern Carolina
10. Discussion of Asbury Church and the cemetery.
11. Asbury and the moving of William Townsend's grave to

Asbury Church.

12. Research in Robeson Co. Research on Daniel T. of Charleston, B.C.
Johnson of Wake Co.

13. Kate Biggs records and the disproving of Daniel of Charleston, S.C.

14. Repetition of Daniel of Charleston, C.C.

15. Redundancy, horrid grammar, - Daniel of Charleston, S.C. & Kate Biggs.

16. Discussion of my article not accepted by STATE mag. Discussion of Thomas of Cumberland- redundancy Lakeview, S.C. Townsends

17. R.I. or Conn.? Is that the Lakeview Connection?

18. Discussion of authenticity of Thomas T. Sr. of Cumberland, wills and deeds

19 Discussion of Thomas T. will in Cumberland. What does it prove?
Deeds in McConkey family
Back to Kate Biggs's records again.

20. More discussion of Kate Biggs records. Research in England on Richard of Va., Lord John Townsend, the Scottish flow, Carver's Creek Quakers. Society of Friends.

21. My sister in Kansas- Rita Townsend. Quaker research on Carver's Creek in London-more details

22. MTR: diaries and notes from own ancestors. Discussion of Daniel's autobiography. The house at Raynham, England.

23 Discussion of Townsends over the years going to Raynham and the nuisance it must be to those Townsends

24. The law of primogeniture- first born gets it all. Is MTR

tired of the research- no? County historical societies in England Research in Island- Barbados, etc. Then Richard of Va. again.

25. Our Va. family connections that moved to Robeson- not Townsends

Charles Townshend, Exchequer of England

26. Early settlement of Bladen direct from England or Scotland. [The end of Matilda "Tilly's Notes" to Daniel,'82]

Matilda Townsend Ruffin left me with her legacy, image, and mindful of her energy to locate Thomas' father.

Chapter Five

Selected Letters from TSA and Cumberland Library

Dear Daniel,

Thanks for the invitation to meet with you and others on December 20th. I am sure that I can't make that date; it being so close to Christmas and I shall already be far to the south.

However, I am planning to attend the TSA meeting on October 30th in New York. From there we will be heading south on I-95. Our first stop will be in Newport News, Virginia where our eldest son lives. We never know our exact time schedule there, as it is sometimes hard to break away from the grandchildren. But, while I am there I shall give you a call. Maybe we could meet for a long lunch or even dinner over which we might discuss your problems in genealogy.

I truly appreciate your sincere efforts but possibly you have the cart before the horse, as the old saying goes.

You will not find Quaker records in England or any other place such as Scotland, Ireland or Wales. George Fox founded The Society of Friends circa 1650. They were an abomination to the official churches, as in England that would be the Church of England or Episcopalian. Hosts of Quakers were jailed for being dissenters. When the jails were full there had to be a solution. The easiest solution was to deport them. That is why in searching early manifests of ships that carried persons to the American Colonies so many persons are listed as "Transported". They were sent. Emigrants who paid for their own passage are listed as "Emigrated". Any one Quaker may or may not have been happy about being sent to the colonies.

I am sure that you know that even the now famous William Penn served times in prison for being a Quaker. He faired better than most simply because he belonged to a privileged class in England.

In Massachusetts (founded as a Puritan Colony) Quakers were whipped and even burned at the stake. They were banished from that colony and most ended up in Rhode Island, the islands off the coast of Rhode Island and on Long Island.

The three Townsend brothers were jailed and fined for being Quakers or sympathizing with Quakers while living under Dutch rule in New Amsterdam *and Flushing, Queens County, New York. In short, Quakers were a hated lot by churchmen everywhere.*

Any good library will provide you with some good old horror books on Quaker persecutions both in this country and in Europe. I simply tell you all this because American Quakers would not have sent any records home to England nor did England wish to hear anything more about them.

Of course, in time the Quakers did get a toehold in England and any records there would deal with those persons in that country.

Quakers are hard to trace by nature of their religion. They got thrown out of some of the best places and they also moved a lot by choice. History would indicate that they went in groups, mostly related, to settle in the wildest of wilderness. But as soon as their area was found and began to settle up they felt threatened and would move on.

All is not lost. Quakers did keep good records and they can be found. If not all of them, then fragments of them.

Carver Creek was apparently a Meeting. As a Meeting it belonged to a Monthly Meeting. A Monthly Meeting had to belong to a Yearly Meeting. A Monthly Meeting would cover great distances and would take unto itself numerous Meetings. A Yearly Meeting would cover even greater distances and would take unto itself numerous Monthly Meetings.

Somewhere in your own area you have to find the data on the Monthly and Yearly Meeting to which Carver's Creek belonged. The records are with all of the different parts of the Quaker Meeting structure. By distance I mean that and you will surely be surprised.

There is an old Quaker Meeting called Nine Partners in New York. To my amazement I found that Vermont and New Hampshire and parts of Canada belonged to the New York Yearly Meeting.

William Wade Hinshaw printed numerous volumes of Quaker Records. Volume I records 33 of the oldest Meetings in North Carolina. Volume II records 4 oldest Meetings in

Pennsylvania and New Jersey. Volume VI records Meetings in Virginia.

I don't know if Carver's Creek belonged to the New Garden Monthly meeting or not but the records of that Monthly Meeting (1752-1770) are in print. Reference: COLLECTION OF SUFFERINGS OF THE PEOPLE CALLED QUAKERS, Joseph Besse. This book covers England (Vol. 1) Massachusetts, Barbados and Virginia (Volume II). Indexed by counties.

The English Quaker Records are in the Gilbert Cope Collection, Genealogical Society of Pennsylvania, and Philadelphia. They cover the English records from the founding of The Society of Friends up to the year 1725. So don't pay anyone to look for things in England that are already in this country, should you ever need them.

I have an idea that you know more about your elusive ancestor than you think you do. Perhaps, if you are willing, I can show you a system by which to M work. It was taught to me and has proven to be worth its weight in gold over the years. It is very easy to learn and it will surely help you if you can get other interested parties to pitch in. You will know exactly what to assign for homework.

Hope to see you soon.

Sincerely,

Martha Burke, Genealogist~

Townsend Society of America, Oyster Bay, New York

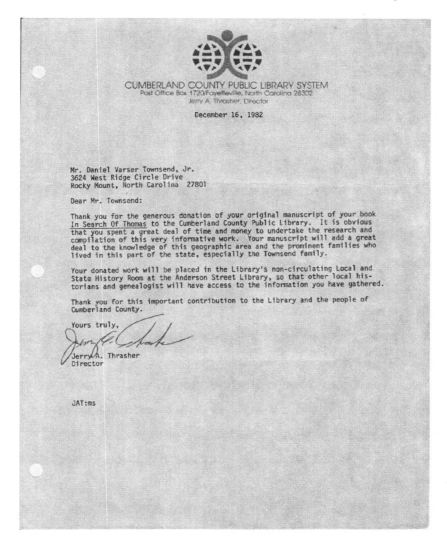

CUMBERLAND COUNTY PUBLIC LIBRARY SYSTEM
Post Office Box 1720/Fayetteville, North Carolina 28302
Jerry A. Thrasher, Director

December 16, 1982

Mr. Daniel Varser Townsend, Jr.
3624 West Ridge Circle Drive
Rocky Mount, North Carolina 27801

Dear Mr. Townsend:

Thank you for the generous donation of your original manuscript of your book In Search Of Thomas to the Cumberland County Public Library. It is obvious that you spent a great deal of time and money to undertake the research and compilation of this very informative work. Your manuscript will add a great deal to the knowledge of this geographic area and the prominent families who lived in this part of the state, especially the Townsend family.

Your donated work will be placed in the Library's non-circulating Local and State History Room at the Anderson Street Library, so that other local historians and genealogist will have access to the information you have gathered.

Thank you for this important contribution to the Library and the people of Cumberland County.

Yours truly,

Jerry A. Thrasher
Director

JAT:ms

CUMBERLAND COUNTY PUBLIC LIBRARY SYSTEM
Post Office Box 1720/Fayetteville,
North Carolina 28302
Jerry A. Thrasher, Director

May 13, 1982

I

Mr. Dan V. Townsend, Vice-President
Harris-Cuthrell, Inc.
Post Office Box 673
Rocky Mount, North Carolina 27801
Dear Mr. Townsend:

This is to confirm our conversation of May 12, in which we discussed the donation of your genealogical notebook on the Townsend family, entitled In Search Of Thomas.

The Library would be most pleased to accept the donation of your research findings on the Townsend family for our North Carolina Reference Room. As you pointed out the Townsend name appears in Cumberland County history as early as 1725. Your work is sure to be of interest to other local genealogists in the Cape Fear Valley area.

As I mentioned over the telephone, our policy prohibits the Library from giving a cost evaluation of donations. I am enclosing a copy of the Library's donation policy for your reference.

I look forward to reviewing your research and adding it to our collection.

We might also keep in mind the possibility of a news release or even a photograph with the local newspaper about the donation.

Let me know if I can be of any further assistance.

Yours truly

Jerry A. Thrasher, Director
Cumberland County Library,
Fayetteville, 1982

Chapter Six

Kate (Townsend) Biggs

Much research on the Townsend family in Robeson County was done by Mrs. F. K. (Britt) Biggs. Her research and conclusions are in Lumberton Library. Her son is Murchison Biggs. I have written to her son, a former Mayor of Lumberton in Robeson. I have never heard back from him. Per Matilda, she allegedly was going to burn her research before her death. This section of reproductions is some of her *records. (Picture from Old Newspaper**.)

For years Kates work in Robeson County was that of a leader in family research. As a Townsend expert, she claimed the family line was of the Thomas of Lynn Mass line, but some found the dates conflicted with logic. Matilda found that Daniel of Edisto would have to have been twelve years of age when he fathered Thomas. Daniel was said to have been in Edisto at age 30 in 1688 as I recall, and Thomas date of birth was 1725 so I am not certain of this concern.

Chapter Seven

Planning the Pilgrimage to old Raynham England

As I continued to think about my family roots I believed a trip to England was necessary. Some felt I should seek out Quakers in London, others felt that Raynham Hall might have answers. Some believed that news from the English side might be better than from our American side which was often devastated by fires and colonial decay that dominated our land for 150 years after 1607. I wanted to go and see just why Townsends left England, and who may have been Thomas' ancestors, my ancestors.

It was a sunny day, the 25th of the month, just past the "Ides of March". The temperature in Eastern Carolina climbed close to sixty degrees. My plans to visit East Anglia in the United Kingdom continued and my hope for finding new information about Thomas grew with each day that brought me closer.

I experienced both fear and anxiety as the time grew near for the overseas voyage to County Norfolk.

Prior to the Pilgrimage, what do we know for sure?

During the past year, there had been so many hopes that were dashed as a result of frustrated leads that did not pan out. It appeared recently that all the evidence pointed towards Charleston, South Carolina with the historical landing in 1630 of Andrew and Daniel, children of Thomas of Lynn, Massachusetts.

Having visited Edisto Island and Wadmalow and other such places such as the South Carolina Historical Society, I now find my hopes a little bit more dashed. The issue of that Daniel's birth date, and a lack of genealogists whom I have contacted in Charleston combine to stifle me. It seemed that the few have a full workload due to the continuing popularity of family tree work.

Obviously, we are able to uncover a number of wills that are interesting. Daniel of Charleston is buried there and had children, one of whom was William. It is a good possibility that William's children who are the missing link.

Some hope was built around the possibility of Andrew Townsend, probably Daniel's older brother. However, we have recently received information from a Townsend Genealogy publication from Leland H. Townsend that Andrew is buried in New England.

So again, we face the ups and downs of the search. Visits to the Fayetteville Courthouse, the Cumberland Library and the Library in Lumberton have offered us very little although I continue to make new contacts while looking for fresh answers.

This past weekend William F. Townsend, my younger brother, and I spent Saturday looking for old graveyards in southeastern Cumberland County based near Grannis Airfield in Fayetteville. While we found many graveyards, we were unable to find any substantial graveyards with markings of Townsend or McConkey. We did find that the Cape Fear Baptist Church, southeast of Fayetteville, does have a number of Townsends buried there, but most seem too recent. The Church office was not open so we were unable to ask for a registration or old graves in that site.

I have also written the Archives in Raleigh regarding other possible old cemeteries, specifically the Dunn Quaker Cemetery which is twelve and one half miles southeast of Fayetteville and the site of numerous meetings of early Quakers. This is the site of a graveyard as well.

While in Fayetteville, I spent time securing a passport for my overseas travel. The process was a bit more complicated than I had expected. Obtaining my birth certificate, international driver's permit and weight limits were hurtles for me. I wanted to take photographs, cameras, and taping equipment for the data-seeking trip.

I have made one final effort to get a response from the Marquis Townshend of Raynham Hall. I wrote him that I hoped he would receive me and that this would be my final correspondence prior to my departure from Carolina April 14,1982.

Interestingly, I left Rocky Mount about 1:00 PM on and arrived Heathrow Airport in London about ten hours later. It is amazing that this trip that could be made so quickly, used to take over six weeks by ship from England via Africa and the Caribbean Island winds. There is not nearly the investment of time as there use to be, but then time today is so compacted anyway.

Prelude to my visit: Colonial Carolina

I recall that the English brought problems on themselves in the Carolina experiment. Because they had a Charter that said they could have black slaves, they loosened that interpretation to include Indians. Having stolen Indian children from their homes, they were constantly being raided and pillaged by the Tuscarora. The Tuscarora, in retaliation, took delight in killing as many whites as they could find who came upstream on the Cape Fear River or the Black River fork from Brunswick, the site of the English settlement at the mouth.

Each time a ship would venture upstream, the mouth of the Cape Fear, the Tuscarora would hang around the banks and swim out to the ship to sink it and maim and kill all the inhabitants.

Also, Black Beard (Edward Teach, or Edward Beard) with his pirate henchmen hung around the Frying Pan Shoals entrance to the Cape Feare River, which prevented anyone but lunatics or bold navigators from trying their hand at the Cape Fear. During this period, around 1716's and before, the English preferred to make settlement at Virginia around Norfolk and the James River. In addition they settled Charles Towne, which later became Charleston.

In those days, the American newcomers used the rivers as we use roads today. They thought nothing of going hundreds of miles by boat. They would sail up and down the coast and make new settlements.

My grandfather once closed his dry good store in Robeson and sent a post card back home saying, " in Havana having a wonderful time, see you soon", Frank. "Water was the road of the 1700s, 1800s and early 1900s."

Eventually, a number of things allowed for the development of Robeson and Cumberland Counties. Finally, the English were fed up with the Tuscarora raids and called for their allies in South Carolina, New York, and Virginia to come down and help fight the Indians. The Tuscarora were badly beaten and limped off to what became their permanent refuge in New York State.

The Scottish Civil War was one of the bloodiest in history. The atrocities experienced in the Highlands by brother against brother and English against Scottish were unparalleled.

Following the defeat of the Scottish and the breakup of their clans and the taking of their lands, the Scottish elected to try their luck at the New World.

One Scottish ship made it past the perils of

Black beard, Frying Pan Shoals, and the Tuscarora and stopped before they arrived up river at the river port, Cross Creek near Fayetteville. Having endured many hardships, early Scotch immigrants petitioned the Province of North Carolina for tax relief. The North Carolina Assembly was impressed with the fact that these brave immigrants had endured so many hardships and they did finally agree to grant tax immunity to the Scottish settlers.

Moreover, they advised the Scottish Highlanders that any other Scottish ship with one hundred or more immigrants would be given land and tax-free status for a ten-year period. When word of these good terms reached Scotland, immediate preparation was made to go to the New World.

Within a very short span of time, over 150 ships of Scottish Highlanders poured across the Atlantic to make the six-week voyage to Cross Creek. The arrival of the McDonalds and all the other Scottish clans created in effect a new Scotland in the Cape Feare Basin about 1747.

It was about this time that our Thomas Townsend and William Townsend ancestors found their way to Robeson County. Whether they came as a result of land grants or merely as opportunists, or in search of the hand of a fair maiden, no one really knows. We do believe that Thomas married Alexander McConkeys daughter, Letisha. We also believe that one of the first records of Thomas and a remote kinsman, Solomon, appeared at the Spanish Alarm in 1748.

The Spaniards were not aware of a peace treaty with England and they captured the British ship Loretta near the mouth of the Cape Fear, sailing it into the port-settlement of Brunswick. They besieged the Brunswick towne's people and drove them inland for several days before returning to their ship in a drunken state.

The Brunswick settlers returned to the village and in great anger began to fight against the Spaniards with whatever they could find. The Spaniards decided to open-fire on the settlement again but by a stroke of fate the gunpowder magazine on the Spanish ship exploded, sinking all hands into the water.

The Brunswick settlers evidently were eager to greet the Spaniards as they swam ashore because they enslaved the Spaniards for the remainder of their lives. The townspeople also swam out to the sunken ship and salvaged gold, silver, and famous paintings. All the booty from the sinking of the Spanish ship in the Spanish Alarm of 1748 made Brunswick one of the richest towns in the New World.

One of the ship's large paintings from the Captain's cabin hangs in one of the old Saint James Church in Wilmington today.

It appears that the two Townsends, Thomas and Solomon, were in the company of John Ashe during this alarm. The other Spanish ship was allowed to sail free out into the open ocean and away from Brunswick, never having realized that the short war was a violation of a new treaty with their country and England.

Some believe that Thomas Townsend and Letisha were part of the Quaker movement, which was predominant in eastern North Carolina. Carvers Creek and Dunn's Creek were sites of many Quaker meetings; however, the minutes of these meetings have been destroyed. I wrote to England in search of copies of these minutes, which according to contacts at Guilford College were returned to England, intact. If we can find the minutes of Carver's Creek Quakers Meetings, we might determine a little bit more about the true identity of Thomas of Cumberland and his family in the New World. At any rate, the search continued as no response provided helpful news.

We have been frustrated with locating settlements of ancient wills. While we have had a good deal of success in locating wills which name children, there is no settlement to give us specifics of the children. We only have names. This creates considerable confusion because we may be dealing with two, three, or even four Thomas Townsends during the same period, or we could be dealing with one. Family Bibles were at times good sources of valid data. The use of family bibles was predicated on a Christian family, a literate family-member, and a recorder who had the will to records births and deaths, for years. Kathy Townsend provided this example of her father's family bible, which is ragged, and torn. It dates back to the 1850's and has excellent records, although there are no entries into that bible after 1940!

Kathy's 1910 Family Bible: see pix pg. 125

It is confusing because there are so many documents and so little historical determination. Unfortunately, these early Americans could not write well, were not well educated, and did not keep many records.

Raynham Hall, U.K.

Chapter Eight

An Expanded Look at Our English Roots

1982 Memoirs of the trip:

Recorded: *Today is my first full day in England, and I am speechless. It's just unbelievable---- It's beyond my wildest dreams----it's as bright as any Carolina morning. The people, the weather; it's just fantastic. The sun is out, and I have been for a jog by the River Wemsley in Norwich. Flowers are in full bloom, streets are busy, Jonquils, as wells as small plants are plentiful.*

It is about 7:30 A.M. and the streets are busy with bikers, cars, and walkers! More people seem to be riding bicycles or walking to work than back home. They are all dressed in coat, dress, and the like. I planned to go over to Norwich Airport.

I am going over to the Regional Airfield. I met a couple of people yesterday who invited me to come by for a cup of tea this morning, and I am going to take them up on it. I am just elated. This is the finest feeling. I am just elated.

Left-handed driving is really something. Everything is in the left hand. It is my hope that some Brits will agree to a tape-recording and engage in conversation.

Dan Townsend points to English Coat of Arms
upon arrive in Great Britain in 1982

All the planes in Norfolk appear to be prop planes. It looks very much like a stateside rural airport, such as Hickory, North Carolina or Lancaster, Pennsylvania.

Well, I went into an English grocery market and bought some groceries. It was interesting. It's a little bit more expensive than I'm used to. The bread is on the shelf without wrapping, exposed to the elements.

I am trying to drive to Fakenham from here, and I'm having difficulty with the cultural mores being so different. Downtown Norwich reminds me a great deal of Charlotte. traffic is hideous. It seemed to flow better this morning; it's treacherously busy now.

I had trouble finding a laundry due to the names and lack of signage. I was basically on the outs. In fact, I have had trouble doing everything in County Norfolk. I had trouble using a pay phone because first of all, I could not figure out what a 10-pence was. Then when I figured what a 10-pence was, I could not get it to go into the phone. But eventually I was able to make a phone call, with some help.

I met Gillian Norman Sharp, Norwich Airport receptionist, and the owners of the B&B where I will be staying, and they all were more than cordial. I think the B&B owner is a machinist or metalist. His wife made breakfast each day in Norwich.

There are some American stores here: Texaco station here on my left. I have seen a Shell gas station, but not a lot of American products. Since my present job is with Converse athletics, I am most interested in distribution throughout the United Kingdom. Almost no one has heard of Converse Athletic shoes, it seems. In fact, I have not met anyone yet that who has. I will meet a distributor in Bath, England in a later trip about who distributed Converse, but not on this initial this trip.

The police cars are the famous German brand Mercedes Benz, white with a bright orange stripe down the side. Wow! There are crazy traffic "islands", or circles. It was told to me that the British favor round-a-bouts in lieu of traffic lights, perhaps these are one of those mentioned. I saw some of those double-decker red buses. There were people sitting on top-level, in the open air, which seemed odd to me.

*The Brits are scurrying to and from on bike, minis, and walking. They seem industrious. There are lots of bicycles. The climate is outstanding. I am totally shocked. The temperature is around 60° degrees, but you know these Brits say it is 26, since they measure in Celsius. Plus, on the **tele,** they say the weather will be mostly fine, to fine, what ever that means?*

Finally, I am traveling to Fakenham, County Norfolk. I was told it would take twenty minutes, and there is no posted speed limit! I am on the open highway. I just passed an Exxon station and the price of gasoline was 1.56 per liter, which translates to just about $2.70 a gallon [1982]. I saw my first pheasant on the highway; it looked like a skinny chicken, but with purple plumes.

As I arrive Fakenham and it is agricultural flatland. It appears like New Zealand pastureland or magazine photograph. There are lots of rocks amidst the green. I wonder where Raynham Hall will be. Winding roadways lined with trees, but beyond that first little row of trees, all I see is wide-open fields. There is flock of sheep. This land appears 'old'. The soil is blacked with age, the rocks rounded, the mounds timeworn. There is greenery is everywhere—in the trees, shrubs, and flora. There is a roadside twenty-foot high stack of hay, perhaps was animal feed?

I pass a couple of quaint, thatched-roof homes; but one or two would qualify as mansions. Those appeared to be old stone, perhaps quarried hundreds of years ago, aged, and worn by time, rains and storms.

One other observation that I would make about the people is that everyone I approach to ask a question, whether a man or a woman, or even a child, is courteous. If they see me walking towards them, they come to me. They go into great detail as far as the instructions regarding what I want to achieve in Britain.

Upon finding a gas station attendant, *I asked," where I could find Raynham Hall." The attendant responds with the British tongue:*

"Other sides of Fakenham turn left."~ I ask, "How many miles would you guess it would be, out that way?"

~ "Six miles."

No one asks you any silly questions like "Are you an American?" They just treat you with dignity as if you are a local citizen. That is relatively impressive. American's visiting must realize they are on foreign soil, not in Carolina or whatever state any longer!

The gas is six pounds, 46 pence to fill the tank on my hired red mini, with 13" wheels.

At the Constabulary (i.e. police station):

"Hello. I am from America and I would like to get some information on the Raynham Hall Townsends down the road. Is there a captain or chief here?"

~"We do not have anyone here at the moment."

"What about a mayor or councilman's office?"

~"Yes. If you go straight down this road." She said, pointing at a road.

"*That sounds fine. Do most people take lunch from twelve to one?*"

~"*Sometimes from one to two. There is usually someone over there anyway.*"

"*Do you have a town mayor? Who is the head of your government?*"

~"*I am not really sure, but they would probably know. Somebody is the head.*"

I have just been into the police office, and the Captain was not there. I have to go down to the Council.

It seems to be a quaint little town even though the streets are narrow. There is hardly any room for a car let alone all these people who are walking around. I still do not see Raynham Castle or buildings I recognize from readings. The streets are jammed; there must be three or four hundred people walking along the side of my car.

There is an outdoor market and I feel the need to take pictures of it. I don't think I have ever seen streets quite as crowded as downtown Fakenham. It looks like an outdoor Mardi gras—an outdoor street gala, festival, market, carts, and people mingling about seemingly rubbing into the hired car.

) **Religious Society of Friends**

FRIENDS HOUSE EUSTON ROAD LONDON NW1 2BJ   **Telephone: 01-387 3601**

Recording Clerk Geoffrey Bowes   *Assistant Recording Clerk* Christopher Thomas

---

Library
Librarian Edward H. Milligan

16.iv.1982

Dear Daniel Townsend

      Thank you for your letter of 31 March, inquiring about the records of
Carver's Creek and Dunn's Quakers. I am sorry to say that we know nothing of
the records of these meetings. If they were returned to England (something of
which we were not aware), these records did not come to us. We do possess
birth, marriage and burial records, but only for Great Britain; the inclosed
leaflet on sources will give an idea of the range. We also have the local records
for London & Middlesex, but most other records are held locally in Great Britain.
We possess no original American Quaker records.

                                  Yours sincerely

                                pp Margaret Kohler

Daniel Townsend
3624 Westridge Circle Drive
Rocky Mount NC 27801 U S A

Comments upon seeing Raynham Hall, County Norfolk

*I think I see Raynham Hall! It sits on thousands of acres.
Could that be Raynham Hall? My Lord! It is! I know it is! It is
behind those trees.*

Sign says, *"East Raynham, Please drive slowly."*

*With the first glimpse of the majesty of Raynham Hall, I
would recognize the structure of that building anywhere. I must
be miles from it. It is an awesome, physical structure. First, there
is a small rustic village. Then, there are some distant gates here at
Raynham Hall through which I am driving my rented mini.*

*So I was to see what happened next. I am sure that this was
Raynham. It just cannot be any other place. I'd bet my life on it.*

Such anticipation and eventful saga!

Inside the gates there are security quarters on each side. I ease down this long, long driveway, which appears to be a mile or so long. Jonquils are abloom, birds singing.

The slow drive reminds me of Reynolda Gardens in Winston-Salem or parts of Arlie Gardens of Wilmington in bloom. Raynham Hall is statuesque, really magnificent. My Lord! It even has a Church of its own. I am little spellbound. It is as if I'm seen my dream unfold, a fairy tale come true.

There are thousands and thousands of jonquils. It looks much like Duke Chapel off to the left. Perhaps the Townshends are at home. We shall very soon find out. I am going to feel an awkward and nervous to the bone.

I don't seem to get an answer at the massive front doors. The doors are much like some old castle doors from movie sets. So, I l walk around the manor to the garden where there are some gardener's working. I do not have any idea of what to expect. Here is how my hand tape recorder tapes the visit.

- *"Good Morning! Beautiful day isn't it?"*

Closest gardener, *"Yes."*

I say, - *"My name is Dan Townsend, and I am from America. Are any of the Townsends in today?"* Gardener, *"No, I am afraid they have gone to New Market."*

- *"When do you expect them to be in?"* I asked.

"Come this way. He utters, the first day back after Easter Monday, there was snow here."   I note he speaks with a strange English accent as I follow. I say,

- *"You would never know it today. I parked around front, do most people park around here?"*

"This is where our visitors usually park."

- *"Should I follow you back?"*

"Yes." He led me though endless building catacombs and emerged in a large kitchen filled with a dozen women. Then disappears into the central foyer while I was left standing. Just then a sophisticated a fine lady approaches.

- *Hi. I said*, forgetting my manners.

"Hello." She speaks with such precision and maintains such a polished accent.

"Thank you very much", I said softly as the gardener left the room.

"Excuse me, are you Mr. Townsend?" A young, aristocratic and accented young lady inquires. She descended from spiral stairs. She approaches, and continues:

"I am afraid this is a private house so we can't really let people around it."

"Are you his secretary?

"Yes." The Marques is 'private'. She said,

"I sent you a letter. It must have crossed over. We have had trouble with the post lately. Did you receive it?"

"No.", I am afraid not. But,

Are they going to be in at all this week?"

"No, they are away. They are in Somerset."

~ "Might it be possible to speak with you for a few minutes?"
I asked.

*"Yes. We will need to go downstairs. I should not let anyone
into the house."*

I was taken by her manner and loveliness as we moved to
her lead. I inquire:

~"Have you been the secretary here for a while?"

"A couple of years."

~"Are you native of the Raynham area?"

"Ten miles away. They are away quite a lot."

*~ "I know they have probably over the years had a lot of
Townsends trying to see them," I say.*

*"There is no end to Americans who sort of think because they
are a 'Townsend' that they are related. I do not know the family
history, but I think there are General Townsends. I think General
Townsend Howe is a cousin of a sort, but everybody else is far
removed. Lord Townshend likes to keep his privacy."*

*~ "I can understand that. Are the family names the same?
Was it Lord Durham at one time?"*

"I am not sure."

~ "Is Agnes still here?"

*"No, there is a Miss Victoria who is a cousin of Lord
Townshend, who lives down in a nearby village."*

~ "Did Lord Marques happen to receive the tape that I sent?" I asked.

"Yes, he received it. Marchioness, or Lady Townsend, listened to the tape. They went to America in February."

"They have some friends in the Townsend Society there, do they not?"

"I think General Townsend Howe is."

~ *"Well, I had no unrealistic expectations. I have just really wanted to see Bracon. Where would Bracon Ashe be?"*

"It is in Norwich. That of course is seat of Norfolk"

~ *"Some twelve or thirteen Townsend families originated in this greater County Norfolk area. I guess back to 1066."*

"Yes, they go back a long way."

~ *"In our particular line, there are a good many who believe that Thomas of Lynn, who was related to this line,*

Had a son who moved from New England to the Carolinas. I believe there was a Daniel, also an Andrew, so that is where we were tying in; through their children originally of Massachusetts, then to North Carolina."

"Yes, you get so many branches back then."

~I ask Jayne" How do your pronounce 'Marques?'"

"Marcus."

~ *"What is the female version of that title?"*

She says," *Marchioness."*

~ *"Is it similar to a French term of that name?"*

"Yes, Lord Townshend spells it Marques, rather than the Marquis."

~Inquiring, I question," *Is he a tall man?"*

"*Yes.*"

-"*How tall would you guess? 6'2"?*

"*6'4"*, she responds.

-"I will not take much more of your time. I know that you are busy."

"*It is pretty frantic at the moment.*" says Jayne

-*I say,* "*Do Marques and Lady Townshend ever receive people from the States?*"

Jayne says, "*Not normally, no. It is just where you draw the line. If you say yes to one, then why shouldn't you say yes to all?*"

-"I can understand that. Is he active in the Government in London?"

"*No, not at all. I think he was active in politics, but now he has so many other outside interests that he really does not have any time for that.*"

- "*If I wanted to just send him some information to your attention to whom do I send it?*"

"*Jayne Kilbert.*"

- "*Is there a better address than just Raynham Hall? What is that zip code here?*"

"*NR21 7OP. But the postman knows where we are.*" County Norfolk, England.

"*Well, I am certainly enjoying my trip. I do not think I would have done myself justice if I hadn't at least tried to come over here. I would like to take a few pictures of the grounds. Is that acceptable?*"

"The general rule that Lord Townshend says is that he does not want people wandering around."

"Do you have a kind of Townsend Society in England?"

"There is something called Balls Townsend Society, but that's because it is based at Balls Park which was where another English Townshend family resides. It is a small society, the Balls Park group."

"How do you spell that?"

"Balls Park, Hertfordshire. It has nothing to do with this family, and of course, the Townshend family used to own Balls Park. Therefore, they can use the Townshend name to call the Society that name. That is the only relationship between his name and the Society."

I continue," *This must be terribly exciting work for you."*

Jayne says," *I enjoy it, yes. It is very gratifying."*

I wish to know," Do you plan to stay in England your whole life?"*

Jayne, "*Oh yes, but I have had many trips abroad."*

"Where have you traveled?"

Jayne replies," *France and South Africa."*

"I bet that's nice. What do you think of the Falkland Island thing?"

"It is a mess."

"Is Margaret Thatcher's job on the line?"

"Oh, I don't know."

I ask," *Lord Carrington did resign, did he not?"*

"Yes. "

I conclude, *"I hope they get it straightened out, and quick. I conclude, I really do appreciate your time."*

"Rules are rules," she said.

"No problem at all with it. I would not have felt comfortable or at peace with myself if I had not come. I am writing a book," said I.

Jayne, " Lord Townshend, I'm sure, would be interested in that."

"It's pretty much a documentary." I exclaimed.

Jayne," I have noticed from tape you sent that you have researched hard into family Townsend history."

"Yes", I inquired, *"Is there more than one Coat of Arms for this family?"*

Jayne, "I don't know."

Concluding I say, *"Well, I would like to leave my card for him and tell him that I appreciate the opportunity to be able to come make inquiry. Thank you."*

Jayne," Pleasure."

I exited through the rear exit of the Raynham Hall complex. I don't know how large this Raynham actually is, but it is enormous. Constructed in 1400 by Inigo Jones the site is home to the French Normans who conquered the lands after English King Harold lost at Hastings in1066. Toushende or "Towns Enders" became the dominant family name for the Lord of East Anglia, and this land across the sea from Belgium has been ruled since about 900 by the same lines, minus the French Normans.

The architectural buttresses make the Hall-Castle stand out in 600 years of history, and timeless in memories. Many of these are recorded in books of the ages.

During my visit, Jayne has given me an explanation and apparently Lord Townshend really does cherish his privacy (pronounced "pri-vi-cie"), even more than I imagined. He is apparently caught up in extensive worthwhile projects to do with the English Society and has made no more trips abroad. So I am going to try to snap a couple of quick pictures as I return to my hired, mini car. This is the ultra "Mini" hired car in England circa 1981.

That is a long way for a trek to Raynham Hall. The mansion is a huge colossal in the rural East Raynham countryside. The land is flat similar to eastern North Carolina and as I reflect on the 1400 A.D. structure among the green flatlands, it is austere. A long way from London or even Norwich in County Norfolk, my mini speeds back to Spencer's B&B.

I am back on the road to Norwich. I am trying to examine my feelings having "been there close-up at Raynham". Do I have post-visit feelings doubts, or wishes? Could I in a word capture the spirit of the moment? I suppose it was high adventure of a lifetime—like climbing a mountain zenith. I have read of Townsend's trying to visit and being rebuffed, yet I was there, inside Raynham Hall. I met Marques Townsend's Jayne. I saw the quarters, and halls, and pictures, furnishings, and experienced the long trip over. I had written, sent numerous audiotapes, and itineraries prior to coming.

My trip was anticipated. I did not just show up, unannounced. I was not disappointed. I was in the manor. I was led up through a series of catacombs down into the back entrance and up through the kitchens. The house personnel were busy with chores. Of course, they must have assumed I was family Townsend as opposed to just another American. But Jean (Jayne) was an attractive young lady of about thirty-two years old, met me. She certainly was bright, articulate, and loyal. (Upon revisit in 2007, she is there today working for Marques who has remarried at 87, after to death of the Lady Townsend originally cited in this book).

I took both the 110mm, 8mm colored film, and 35mm pictures, some close up and some from a distance. As I tried to get at a distance to take more pictures, I am sure it was she or her delegate in a car that came up behind my mini. I assumed it was to escort me off the property, when no one pulled out behind me. So I only assumed then that she in fact was escorting me from the property. I took a few more pictures.

I suppose that I am not disappointed. I have been closer to Raynham than others. And there have been so many that have come to England and sought the Townsend identity and have never treaded these steps as I have.

I am eight miles from Norwich, and I suppose more than anything else, I feel happy that the sun was out and that I was even able to take photographs.

It looks like I have plenty of time to do other tourist adventures at Easter Beach Great Yardley Shore, Kings Oysters, and River Wembley boats.

I also want to visit the Norfolk airport again, a travel center. Frankly, now that I am here, I would just about as soon take it easy. I have not really relaxed yet. The trip was much more tiring than I had imagined.

The climate is fine. The food is bland. My Spencer's B & B, breakfast was a poached egg on toast, an English sausage, which had no spice at all, fried tomatoes, a piece of country ham, and four pieces of stone-hard toasted bread with English orange marmalade, and hot tea with cream in it, which I didn't care for at all. It wasn't bad, of course. I like food, as most of the American Townsends do.

It is now 1:45PM in the afternoon on Thursday, April 16, 1982. And with the parting of the clouds, the bright sun has now kicked up the temperature clearly into the mid to high 60's. Hello America, Hello England. We did our best. We did all we set out to achieve with Townshend roots.

Chapter Nine

Peggy's Book, Townsend Research on Townsends

When I initially began searching for Townsend roots in 1979, I was advised of Mrs. John E. (Peggy) Townsend of Route 2, Buie--- tobacco farm community near Red Springs. This was a few miles from Raft Swamp in Robeson County and I had already been to see my childhood friend Bobby Bleeker who owns a Buick dealership in Red Springs, and I knew his Sales Manager from Lumberton. I had always admired how those folk could support a dealership in such a small community.

When I had visited Alexander's line in Red Springs and seen Townsend Drugs and the fantastic mural of Townsend Hotel in the main street. I had been informed of Peggy's work, so I was anxious to meet with her.

When I talked by telephone, with her we agreed that my mother, Alma Louise Sullivan Townsend, and I would visit on a Sunday in her farm home place in Buie. Here we saw first hand how spread out the tobacco business was and just how flat a hundred or so acres could be.

Peggy was a terrific genealogist and offered us a tintype of great, great, grandfather Alfred who was a mutual relative of us both. He was wore a full white bearded which complemented his full white head of hair. She went on to say that the Tyner's and Townsends had intermarried a good bit and she was kin to me on several accounts. It was a good visit and the beginning of a long and fruitful relationship. I mentioned the Townsend's and Tyner's were adjacent one another in Cross Creek cemeteries over in Cumberland county as well.

Peggy went on to inform me of Mrs. Nancy Barnes of Swans Quarter, a village on the North Carolina Coast. It seems that this lady was married to Peggy's family member and could paint the family coat of arms. I jumped at the chance and commissioned seven original coats of arms to be painted for my wife Mary of eighteen years, the each of my four children and several extras that I had framed with different colored borders. They are vibrant, colorful and genuine.

On subsequent visits to Peggy's abode I began to appreciate her son's stamina as he used the family tractor to plow and service the tobacco fields in Robeson as generations of Townsends had done before his time. Her home was quite nice, efficient and traditional for a rural farmstead in Robeson and it is one that I shall forever remember.

Peggy had begun to research old graveyards and vanishing cemeteries. In fact, she told me she was planning a book on this data. Interestingly, I was about looking for the graves of Townsends too. I had my own grave marker hewn in Columbus County and reflects Raynham Hall and the quest for Vassar, my middle name (a name from Robesonian Judge L. Varser). I told Peggy of my visits to the gravesites of William and Ora as well as Roscoe, Grandfather William Frank and Grandmother Mamie Rich Carter Townsend. Also, I disclosed that I had finally found Odom Cemetery, rapidly decaying due to the tombstones being mostly in lightwood; it was the final resting place of our Charles Townsend.

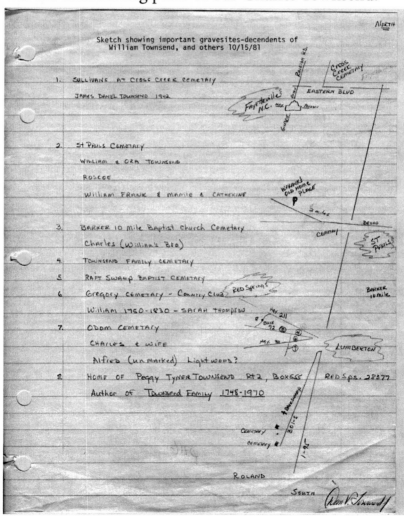

Pictured are gravesites visited by D.V. and Dan in 1982-Handdrawn

I reported that it was unusual that I finally found the ghostly gravesite of William Townsend (and wife Sarah) of 1750 at the Lumberton Country Club. I don't at this time wish to belabor this mysterious point, but apparently Mabel McCall and Matilda Townsend Ruffin had the tombstones removed from this heavily wooded site, undisturbed for hundreds of years, and removed to Asbury Church! The Robeson Sheriff reconciled the movement, and except for the missing Civil War Cross of William of St Pauls grave, all is, as it was. I discussed this with Peggy Townsend who has said she had a hand in the recovery of William and Sarah's tombstones.

As Peggy moved on in her search, I placed my manuscript in the Cumberland County Public Library along with a copy of the Daniel Earle's (Townsend) work of Fort Mill, South Carolina. When I returned to check on my work, D.Earles" had been taken! Removed. Stolen? So, I began to reflect. Perhaps I should remove the local history work even though it was in a non-recirculating status. *It could easily be stolen*, as was perhaps Thomas Townsend's will in 1796, although Peggy said it remains in the archives of Raleigh.

Peggy's work pointed out the Townsend heritage that is clearly marked by the Battle of Hastings in 1066. After the defeat of English King Harold, Louis de Tunneshende was given lordship in East Anglia. He was anxious to stabilize the local Saxons and married into the families there, thus giving a more contemporary last name to family Townshend, or Townsend as it came to be.

The American Colonials scene faced introduced the Stamp Act, or the Townshend Acts in Parliament by Lord Marquis George Townshend of Raynham. Pictured below, is George Townshend who had a lengthy stint in America up to the time of the Revolution. The information is courtesy of the *Landed Baronage of Old England* and was helpful prior to the trip to England.

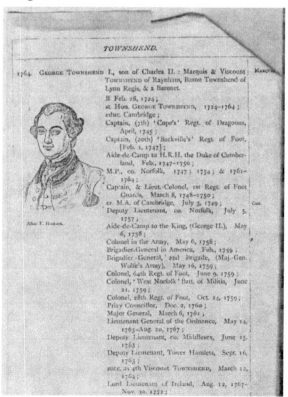

This family dates back to about 900 AD prior to the French incursion. The present facility of Raynham Hall was constructed in 1400 A.D. and attributed to the architect Inigo Jones, with perhaps modern applications in light of Bells of St Mary's improvements of 2005. This author has been inside the structure in 1981 I have made other visits to the family complex.

I tried to wed in the St. Mary's in 1991, but was turned down by letter from the Archbishop of Canterbury. I was informed that I was not a local parishioner and as such I was not entitled to be wed in the Townshend Anglican Chapel on the grounds of Raynham Hall Townshends.

Although I may drift in and out, it seems necessary to address all subjects pertinent to Peggy's work. She went on to point out Bladen County, now Robeson County, records of Thomas, Thomas Jr., William, and their wives, plus the male lines including land or wills of: Alfred Townsend, Charles, William, William Frank, and today we would add Daniel Varser (Vassar) Townsend, Senior; Junior; and III.

Robeson county is home of many Townsend family treasures. It is home to Mrs. Kate Biggs whose work points toward Daniel of Edisto Island, South Carolina.

Thomas Townsend born about 1725, and Peggy points out that Kate Biggs must be wrong or have the wrong dates in her claim that Thomas' father was Daniel of Edisto Island, South Carolina. It seems that Matilda Townsend Ruffin of

Wilson, removed and deceased in Miami, agreed with her. For that assumption to be true held Matilda, "Daniel had to be twelve years of age when he fathered Thomas! Illogical."

Peggy Townsend always encouraged me to look further into the Edisto theory but at that time we lacked relevant information about the Virginia connections that are apparent and detailed today.

Peggy was consumed with being busy or so it seemed in 2006 when I checked on her. Her mother who lived into her nineties passed, and Peggy said she only had time for a few emails. Moreover, she encouraged me to walk cautiously despite my success at presenting the "Southern Townsends" at TSA in Long Island, and despite ancestry.com data locating a William Townsend in York, Virginia. Peggy mostly dealt with traditional proof sources like wills, land grants, marriages, and records. For a century and a half, so many fires and little record-keeping has haunted Townsend's who have researched or sought a connection for Thomas. Perhaps records never existed. So I will search whatever means I find available to seek out probabilities and take the highest percentage choice. No logical answer exists otherwise. So, I shall honor her wishes and not present her findings as a separate chapter in this presentation except to say that The Townsend Family, 1748-1970 by Peggy Townsend has been of great interest to me throughout my own search for Thomas.

Listing of Townsend Couples in our family tree

Thomas Townsend, Sr. (Spanish Alarm)
born in 1725 (Chowan, North Carolina)
died in 1796 near Fayetteville, North Carolina.
m. Letisha McConkey c.1748-1780 Scottish born

William Townsend
b . 4/16/1750 Robeson Co, North Carolina.
d. 7/21/1830 Lumberton (Country Club Golf Course)
m. Sarah Thompson gravesite beside his.

Charles Townsend
b. 4/19/1792
d. 2/12/1829 lightwood marker, Odom Cemetery,
Robeson
m. Martha Blount *Humphrey*

Alfred Townsend
b. 11/12/1819
d. 12/15/1875
m. Edith *Humphrey*

William Townsend (Civil War)
b. 4/22/1842
d. 2/3/1927 St Pauls Cemetery, US Hwy 301-S
m. Orrie Prevatte (French Origin)

William Franklin Townsend
b. 11/21/1882
d. 7/12/1932 St Pauls, Great Depression
m. Mamie Rich Carter, 2nd Wife, Vander, N.C.

Daniel Varser Townsend, World War
II
b. 5/5/1918 Vander
d. 9/21/2001 Fayetteville
m. Alma L. Sullivan, Irish Shoe
Making

Daniel V. Townsend, Jr.
b. 3/16/1944
d.
m. Mary E. Dehmer, Germanic,
New York; Kathy D. Moore,
Lexington, N.C. on April thirteen,
nineteen-hundred, ninety-one.

Daniel V. Townsend, III b.10/4/70
Jennifer Lynn Larkin   b.12/11/72
Michael Bradford   b. 12/17/75
Robert Matthew   b. 8/17/77

Chapter Ten

William & Ora Reunion: July 3, 1982

The first reunion of the descendents of William and Ora Townsend of Saint Pauls, North Carolina was held the third of July 1982, in the Saint Pauls Civic Center, which Lawrence Townsend of St Pauls had arranged. Over ninety men, women, and children descended on the center that was decorated with flowers donated by Alma Sullivan Townsend, wife of D.V. Townsend of Fayetteville; and her son William Frank Townsend. The flowers were on the head table but were carried to the cemetery two miles away for a special memorial after lunch. Jean Townsend Duncan led Townsends to the First Baptist Church for the Sunday morning services the next day.

Daniel Varser Townsend, Jr. served as master of ceremonies. He had prepared large speakers, a public address lectern, a cassette audiotape, and color 35mm slides from his pilgrimage to England in April 1982.

To begin, all were invited to the kitchen area for coffee or soft drinks furnished by Lawrence and Helen Townsend of St Pauls. Many of the early arrivals were given ad hoc assignments as they came in the door. Martha Townsend Kates, her daughter Barbara, Helen Jean T. Duncan, Mary

Dehmer Townsend (wife of DVT, Jr.), Samantha T. Fasul, M. Patricia T. Allen of Vander, Ms. Powers and others too numerous to mention.

Everyone pitched in to get all guests registered with a name tag, and then went through the tough assignment of getting each to complete a family history questionnaire about parents, dates, deaths, and family Townsend data. This process took over an hour as the family filed into the over-capacity civic center in St Pauls.

The day was sweltering with July humidity that made the air-conditioning feel like only a loud noise. I suppose too many folks gathered in the building for humid and hot outside conditions proved an excessive load on the air conditioner's ability to cool.

Daniel V. Jr made several announcements, one that Mr. Wellington was in a Democratic run-off and all would want to consider his candidacy, since he was a family member. Mrs. H. Jean T. Duncan was also recognized for having been elected to a nine county area of public service.

Beginning his opening remarks Daniel, Jr. said, "Welcome kinfolk!" He went on to individually call out the name and city of each who had registered at the door, and some early arrivals that were not registered. He inadvertently overlooked his own parents, Alma and D.V. Sr., his own brother Frank and wife Jane Weeks Townsend and even his sister Pat! No harm was done, for people continued to stream in the back door long after the program began.

After this, the children of William and Ora were mentioned and all of descendents were asked to rise and stand for the special recognition. Berder (Berta) Townsend, pastor of Salem Baptist Church in Winston-Salem in 1930 had almost a dozen attendees; L.H. Lon of St Pauls had eight or nine, Sandy had approximately ten; W. Franklin had twenty-seven; Callie had a crowd of descendents, seventeen or more, many of whom were from the St Pauls - Lumberton area. Ellie's descendents were about a dozen; so all family Townsend groups seemed represented.

There were a few Townsends who were somewhat removed from the lineage but all went back to Alfred of Robeson, one of the men who had a large number of progeny.

William Frank Townsend gave a special invocation to the reunion and cited the significance of the gathering. Afterwards, Dr. Baxter M. Walker, Evangelist and Christian teacher gave a major address on "The Importance of Families in American History. That is Southern History"

"Family," said Dr. Walker, "is what America is all about. A God-believing group of individuals held together with mutual goals and heritage." Dr. Walker had been D.V.'s best friend in life, and was a mentor to Daniel V. Jr. and Frank, as well as to Mrs. Alma Townsend. Dr. Walker interestingly completed studies at Wake Forest University, and earned his PhD. In England with his dissertation on Prayer.

After this, Daniel Jr gave a slide presentation of his Raynham England Visit and played an audio tape of pertinent interviews with Charles P. Carter regarding Mamie Rich Carter Townsend, W. Franklin's second wife and a description of William Roscoe Townsend's drowning at the early age of sixteen on Bullard Mill Pond while his whole seventh grade class and sweetheart (Ms Gaynele Beard) looked on.

Also, there was an interview with Rosalie T. Potter, and several persons in England regarding specific subjects related to "Townsends". These selected recordings gave all attendees a good insight into the attitudes and feelings of family members by persons who "knew" important relics that were memorable to Townsends.

For lunch most of the family went to the east end of St. Pauls to the Golden Skillet; a few went to Hardee's; and a few had to depart town early due to other July 4th obligations. Afterwards, all went to the nearby cemetery and placed William's reconditioned and repainted Confederate Iron Cross (since removed and lost) and flowers on the gravesite of William and Orrie. Huge 4'x2' matted, separate photos of William and Ora had been at the head table during the ceremonies and were taken to the cemetery for the memorial service. D.V. Townsend, Sr offered a special prayer and eulogy to his grandfather, William. Photos were taken there at the

St Pauls Civic Center and were to be made available to those who requested them. Inadvertently, Patricia Townsend-Allen kept the photos after the celebration, and is the caretaker to date.

Lawrence Townsend had some parting words at the cemetery, and several including Douglas, Chief of Police at Blowing Rock made a trek to Gregory Cemetery to see the oldest grave markers of our ancestors, William and Sarah Thompson Townsend. They are buried on the golf course near the Country Club in Lumberton. Their gravestones have been cleaned and they have been there since circa 1830. A story of their removal and restoration is within this book.

Many Townsends came later, like Ora Mae from North Wilkesboro. Some of the dearest souls there were Mildred Townsend Powers in a wheelchair. She resides in a rest home in Lumberton (she was the lady who started D.V. Jr's' quest for the Townsend identity back in the summer of 1981, when the two went through some old news clippings in a cigar box); Rosalie Townsend Potter also came in a wheel chair; E. Thomas "Tommy" Townsend of Wilmington made a brief appearance, though he was actually at a meeting nearby in Fayetteville. Some made a long arduous trip like Ms. Inez Wells Townsend Garner, William Franklin Townsend's surviving (third) wife; as well as Ruth and Joyce Townsend of Winston-Salem. Ora Mae, Martha and Barbara all of the Forsyth County area, who were there to represent Rev.

Berta Townsend's line. Bert Townsend, of Winston, owner of Facts Business Products in Winston-Salem, and his wife also attended.

Personal questionnaires will become valuable for genealogist of the future. At the termination of the day, all were reminded about services at the First Baptist Church on Sunday in honor of the reunion. Also, feedback questionnaires were handed out so that everyone could vote on their preference for the next reunion. Only a handful has responded to date, but most seem to prefer a cooler time of the year, and almost all would like more social time and perhaps a picnic-style lunch. This is what I would expect, given the heat that day

A handful of family members contributed cash to the event for the work, rent of the building, handouts and programs. Several big contributors were Lawrence and Helen of St Pauls, D.V. Townsend Sr of Fayetteville, and Joyce Faw and Ruth T. of the Winston-Salem area.

REFLECTIONS OF YEAR ONE ...

During 1981-1982, I was impressed with so many human factors that affect the Townsends and all Southerners. Some have written that Southerners have a two-fold identity, one having been born in the South and the second from the state of mind, or the spirit, of the Southerners. Indeed Southerners, though many descended from the North or from other parts of the world, have a peculiar history.

This history in growing up in a special social environment has made Southerners distinct and different from the other setters. There is a pride in individualism: Tied to land, farm labor, and family they toiled independently of cities to strike out alone. They developed a unique character, isolated, rural, subsisting on farm food, learning tolerances for each other's plights, and counting on laborers, not machines to do the work. Machines were not the way of Southern plantation or farm life.

Southerners are the only Americans to ever-experienced defeat in battle and defeat in social structure. Southerners cling to tales of their history and to the reality and universality of their perception of wrong. They place a special importance on kinship and the family. In one-way or another, they seem determined to be a religious, impenetrable group of people. Nowhere in America do these traits so classically unveil themselves as they do in the South. It is a regional experience, culture, and history

In examining the family reunion, I am reminded of the many smiles and faces that gathered in the Civic Center. Many of the people on this one-day were full of pride, full of enthusiasm, eagerness, and even anxiousness. I think of the long struggle with egos of those who are involved. Each of us who had a hand in designing the reunion and doing the search for Thomas has our own individual social and cultural needs. Without question, there tends to be a pride of authorship among those from the South, a distinct region, like East Anglia, for example.

From the Civic Center in St. Pauls, North Carolina we reflected upon the ancient home of early Townsend settlers.

Since that grand reunion, I can reflect that there was a genuine warmness on that particular day in July. Many who traveled far under duress, strain, age, or family circumstances came and gathered, bore the temperature, and it was all so natural. There was great acceptance of one another. For a period of time, people put aside anger, frustrations, memories of bad experiences within the family, and as a group, they accepted and shared handshakes, and greetings, broke bread together, they took photographs together, and they made it a momentous occasion for their history and the future.

Perhaps never again will such a complex gathering come together---the invalids in wheelchairs, the young children, the old, those who lived through the Depression, those who founded the First Baptist Church at the home of the Townsends, the brothers, the half-brothers who share only the common father, the ladies, the beautiful, the older, the men, the silver-haired and the dark-haired---the Townsends came in eagerness. They gathered; they celebrated; and they departed.

It is remarkable that such an event could take place, that in just one short year, many driving force could bring together the family whose roots though deep in Robeson soil had carried them to many different vocations and to many parts of our land... from the farmers, to the police chief, to the business people, to the school teachers, to the volunteers.

Perhaps we will never know the significance symbolized in ladies of some of those who gathered, the ladies who were not Townsends until they married. There was Church of England, or perhaps descended from Quakers, Baptists, Presbyterians and seldom Catholics. Those ladies brought the proud heritage of their own into the Townsend name and contributed a great deal of personal qualities of intelligence, perseverance, hard work, forgiveness, and creativity. There are many such names the Wells, the Sullivans, the Powers, the Musclewhites, and, yes, the Prevatte's.

The Townsends think of themselves as a group of Scotch-English but in reality, today the Townsends of the Southeast are a real mixture of time, culture, tradition, and diverse origins. In my immediate family alone there is Scotch, French, English, Irish, and German just to mention some of the women who have blended their bloodlines.

As I gaze at the photograph of those who attended the reunion, I can see the hope of tomorrow in the young that are there; I can see pride of the old who are pleased to be a part of it all. Perhaps for the fleeting moment of the photograph,

I saw a oneness, a great acceptance of who they are, and what they are as a group — one to another, each his own person in the family of the Kingdom of God.

Perhaps in the next fifty years or so, the Townsend family will evolve and leave an even deeper imprint on this great Southeastern region. The simple human wisdom that sprang forth and gave the early settlers the energy to come here surely will drive the family further into the annals of the history of mankind.

CONCLUSIONS 1982

The search for Thomas of Cumberland has been a precious event, yet frustrating. The search occurred during my 37th and 38th year when I was career-minded both at work and at home with four young children and in an executive capacity in a consumer products company, Converse Athletic Shoes & Hanes Sports.

As mentioned, my wife Kathy Moore-Townsend provided a disheveled 1910 bible, which was her father's family back to the 1850's. Provided a literate, dependable, and motivated soul would keep these records they provided great data for generations past, present, and future. Many Bibles have been lost in time-fires.

It would appear that I could draw several conclusions. First of all, most of the research that has been done is virtually exhausted. There are certainly some records, somewhere, that we are not aware of, but most of the genealogists have tired of their quest. My belief is that Richard Townsend sailed from Bracon-Ashe, England in County Norfolk aboard the ship "Welcome" as an indentured servant to Dr. John Potts. Arriving 1621 in James City, Virginia, he served as an indentured servant for a period of time in the art of Surgery and Pharmacy. Feeling that he was not learning enough, he sued Dr. Potts in the Virginia Company environs and was granted his release, and subsequent acreage allotments in the Indian wilderness near Jamestowne.

This Doctor Potts, a hero of sorts in 1725, is memorialized today at Jamestowne settlement with a stone marker in the settlement church citing his service 1621-1635. Back to Captain Richard Townsend as he became known. His family is a famous Virginia family and his sister married George Washington's brother. His two sons, Captain Robert and William, apparently migrated into Albemarle, North Carolina, in the northeastern precincts as it opened around the year 1700. Richard let's remember had landed as in 1621. Richard had sons by the name of William, Captain Robert, and daughter Frances. Robert's son William had a son named William. *This William* had our Thomas, and it is my belief that they continued their migration with the immigrant Virginians and some Scotch further south into northeastern counties and eventually down into the olde Bladen County area.

Leland Townsends book cites this family in 1985 in his book, reflected in Townsend Society of America treatise. Heir

Frances Dade of Texas, who corresponded with us about early Virginia roots or connections to Captain Richard Townsend, and his daughter *Frances*, confirmed it.

The Spanish Alarm of 1747 called coastal colonials including our Thomas Townsend to bear arms for his country, and Brunswicktowne. Following this, it is very likely that Thomas followed the migration of the thousands of Scottish immigrants inland on the Cape Fear, settling in Western-Bladen County, which subsequently became known as Robeson County. Here Thomas Townsend had his family, and we know that he was born 1726 in Chowan County, called then "the Albemarle precinct of Virginia Company settlement" and he died near Fayetteville in 1798. The map shows his lands near Grannis Airfield.

Some have argued that there is a remote possibility that he actually migrated from England to Charleston, South Carolina. Some searches have attempted to tie him to Daniel Townsend of Lynn, Massachusetts, who migrated to Charleston with a brother, Andrew. These families are tied to Raynham Hall in County Norfolk, England. This theory has for the most part been disproved, though the late Kate Biggs of Lumberton, North Carolina espoused it.

A third possibility, yet unearthed and unresolved, is the possibility that Thomas could have come with the Scottish settlers following the battle of Ulster and sailed up to Cape Fear and been an initial immigrant to the Cross Creek area.

Regarding his origin, which will only be found through a divine gift, we know that he had a son by the name of William, who was born April 1750 and died in 1830. He and his wife, Sarah, are buried at Gregory Cemetery at the Lumberton Country Club property. William's son, Charles, was born in April of 1792 and married Martha Humphrey. He had a son, Alfred, who was born in November of 1819 and died October 1893. Alfred married Edith Humphrey. Alfred and Charles are buried at Odom Cemetery off a rural road, approximately seven miles from Lumberton or three miles from the Lumberton Country Club.

Alfred's children were many. One son was William Townsend, who is my great-grandfather. He married Ora Prevatte, and they are buried in the St. Pauls Cemetery, two miles west of the city of St. Pauls, North Carolina, along with some of his children, Berder and William Franklin. I am not certain of the burial site of his daughters and other family members, but the information is provided elsewhere in this manuscript with the family documents that were individually submitted between July 3, 1982 and September 1, 1982.

Chapter Eleven

Incursions of the French

COLONIAL AMERICA

The French have long been associated with their contributions to the Western Hemisphere mankind in general, particularly to the American Revolution. They were competing with the Brits at the time of the Colonial period. The American experience in many ways was a French "survival of the fittest". The French and Indian War showed just how strong the French were in landing a foothold in what we now know as Quebec and Toronto. French pioneers made huge strides along the St. Lawrence seaways in aligning with natives to establish French as a trading language and French practices, colors, flags, and preparation for French modes in a new west.

The French privateers---or pirates, were as plentiful along the Carolina coast as were the Brits and the Spanish. Of course when it came time for the American Revolution, it was the French who stood with the colonist who resisted English taxes.

Statute of Marques de Lafayette+

Most colonists favored Lafayette as the General who stood to lead. He was one of many, including their own Washington. There were also numerous immigrants who came from the countryside of Normandy, such as the Prevatte family who married into the Townsend family in 1750.

Ora Prevatte was only five feet tall and her raven hair is passed on through the genes of her offspring. "Prevatte and Townsend" were both heroes of the Cumberland and Robeson Townsends of North Carolina. Both served as touchstones for one to recall Louis de Toushende who hailed from Normandy prior to Hastings in 1050. He had given the Saxons a French last name, he had laid the path for future French people blended and became a hallmark of the American melting pot, particularly in the Carolinas. The Prevatte's passed on traits including a "widows peak", raven hair, and heavier- framed men. Orrie herself was only five feet tall and all men after her were 5'10", not 6'6" like her husband William. Orrie liked cooking and seemed to foster more fancy home cooking, as any French farmer may have preferred. Her winning ways were prolific into the 21st century by her progenitors whose roots are from Robeson.

Chapter Twelve

D. Earle Townsend of Greenville, SC

I called Earle today for the first time in years. Earle was working home working on his computer and put me on speaker.

Earle and I discussed our work, the Townsend Association's DNA testing, Matilda notes, and our mutual search for Thomas. We spoke of his publication some decade prior in which I purchased the work from him and had attached it to my non re-circulating book in the Cumberland County Ray Avenue Library. It was removed from there! By whom I wondered? Who wanted his manuscript so badly that they would steal his work that I had paid for, and deposited as the second only to my own so that the home of the Townsend will of 1796 would have some local historical reference? It disappeared in 2001, about the time of the World Trade Center attack in New York. I remember the time well.

Earle and I talked of Matilda and of her work in Miami. He said he had made copies of her work kept by her genealogist brother. He went on to say that he had never unraveled the mystery of Thomas' father. Also, he recounted the history of Thomas, Jr's trek to Mississippi in which all five of his sons relocated from Cumberland in the early 1800s or thereabouts.

He next shared his view of the TSA's DNA results he had studied on line from FAMILY DNA in which his DNA, John E.'s, a Pastor in Ireland and mine matched on all twelve points. As Peggy accounted to me some time ago this DNA Group of Townsends is a rather large pool of people although Lewis Townsend or others at TSA have yet to advise me of the results. I learned by the contact with Earle that folks are on their own, even though the program is encouraged by the TSA---Townsend Association of America.

Thomas Townsend's roots were difficult for me to determine. There was the Daniel of Edisto Island, and William of the Virginia Company Precincts. In Baltimore published book about early Virginia settlers, "Tangled Branches and Broken Limbs", I found records of William's land in York and of Thomas, William's son. Items were also found in the will of William, and in future land deals in York.

Apparently Thomas made his way into Carolina with so many such as the Thompson's and other family groups. Thomas came to settle in the Cape Fear basin and met Leticia McConkey whose last name was one of a multitude of Scottish last names, which were invariably spelled differently. I understood this to be a function of the town clerks. Particularly with the Scots, clerks had difficulty writing the names they heard with such a brogue!

Back to Letisha, she came up the Cape Fear with Flora McDonald and 150 ships of Scots after Culloden and began the Carolina experience for the Townsends. I am to talk to Earle later, and to receive more emails from both him and Peggy so I will include any new information that is rendered.

Kingsburgh she repaired to Monkstadt, and during her stay the house was frequented by a great many visitors. It was on this occasion that Lady Margaret made the arrangements for Flora's marriage with Allen MacDonald, Kingsburgh's son.

BARBAQUE CREEK KIRK
(From MacLean's "Scotch Highlanders in America")

Scanned Pix of Flora's Homestead

Acknowledging the book of *Flora McDonald in America*, I note that Flora was born just two years prior to our Thomas. Moreover that Longstreet was popular in 1750 and the river town was called Cross-Creek. They called it Cross Creek as two creeks crossed in village center, and crowds who recognized her as the "Fine Lady of Scotland" saw Flora there frequently. Flora homesteaded twenty miles northwest on a 600-foot hill, Mount Pleasant, now called Cameron. This new town was home to Reverend Campbell who was from Campbelton, Argyleshire, Scotland. This name replaced Cross Creek as the settlement of Highlanders grew. Eventually, the town was named Campbelton, and when the French influenced the Revolution in 1797, it became known as Lafayette Ville.

Flora and other Scot pioneers paved the way for one Solomon Townsend into Anson perhaps, by purchasing 550 acres of Caleb Touchstone. It is eighteen miles north of Rockingham, two miles north of Capel Mills on Mountain Creek, five miles north of Ellerbe Springs. Allen McDonald, Flora's adoring husband, named this pretentious spread Killiegrey. It was intended to be their final dwelling place.

Chapter Thirteen

James Sullivan and James Townsend,

James Sullivan and James Townsend…generations apart led lives that are remarkable and legendary. Both gentlemen proved important in my lifetime.

First there was my mother's brother Jimmy Sullivan, an exuberant man of the thirties and forties, who had attended NC State. He was son to Granddad Jim Sullivan, father of the shoe empire at Ft. Bragg that was sold to the Townsends in 1949.

"James" was an effervescent, outgoing chap, always laughing, with an affinity for movies. He frequented the Carolina Theater and the Colony or sometimes the Miracle theaters on Hay Street during booming downtown Fayetteville growth in the 50's and 60's. He would sometimes go to two movies in the same day, and then pop in on Sis Alma (my mom) at Hay Street Shoe Store, incidentally, where she labored for thirty-five years. He was a consummate salesman, and the pride of Viola Sullivan Bullard of Lafayette Heights, Fayetteville.

Uncle James especially enjoyed the Sullivan-Townsend gathering each Thanksgiving and Christmas family gatherings. Ex-WWII Naval man, Uncle Harry Sullivan, his Long Island-wife Peggy, and their four sons would drive in all-night to see our close-knit family: Coble Wilson, Aunt Virginia, and children Coble Dee, and Patty Wilson son Daniel would drive thirty miles over from Lumberton, and we would drive eight blocks! "We" consisted of D.V. (my dad), Alma, Pat, later Frank, and me. We would join the celebration at the home of my only living grandparent, "Big Mama". Perhaps she was termed that title due to "very heavy" genes inherited from her Indian mother, who was also quite obese and chair-ridden in latter life. Remember "Big Mama's" Dad was the gent whose medicine show rolled into Oklahoma from Carolina each year? Mr. Sullivan, the first had married an Oklahoma Cherokee, Lady "Virginia, Louise, Hepsey, Jane, etc, Summers."(I have her long name recorded elsewhere in this book.)

"James" Sullivan was the life of the family gathering on such holidays, frequently arriving early only to grab a bed and snooze off the night before. Uncle James would awaken in a blast, and noisily greeting everyone, sneaking a piece of caramel cake, my childhood favorite.

His best friend on Woodrow Street at Raeford Road killed James. This oddly was the site of my brother William Frank's first home years later. James was only forty years old when he died. I heard of the shooting, strangely enough, in Winston-Salem on the radio of my freshman dorm in 1963. It was unusual to receive radio news from 135 miles away. I felt shaken and alone, as no one had phoned me. My favorite and best, uncle-friend and Mother's youngest brother, which was James Sullivan, had been tragically struck down.

James "Townsend" was a new friend of late 2006. His family is of lower South Carolina removed to Anderson, Rock Hill, and now Blowing Rock, North Carolina. He ascends from theory one, the Daniel of Edisto Isle, near Charleston in 1718-1747.

Perhaps I am missing one of Daniel of Edisto's sons, perhaps one that is not listed, perhaps one that is without favor, possibly an illegitimate child. Thomas, "our" Thomas born circa 1725-1796 on the Little Pee Dee River out of Georgetown is the missing link.

Now, James Townsend recently told me his own father was missing from key South Carolina records, so it is not impossible. James has a long and noble beginning back to a Thomas from the United Kingdom to Lynn, Massachusetts and his son Daniel I, who left Lynn at age thirty for points south, making his home on Edisto Island.

So, Daniel could have had a missing child, our Thomas, who moved up from the Charleston area, or Charles Towne, up the coast to George Towne toward the Pee Dee River inland to first right on the Little Pee Dee to Bladen, now the Robeson County, Raynham-Lumbee-Raft Swamp area and made it a world where my descendants lived and prospered.

At least until Thomas, Jr's five sons went to the "wild west" of the time, Greenville, Mississippi.

Jim Townsend, or James has a son by the name of Daniel who lives with his wife, a native New Yorker. He was born near the birthday of my son Daniel, in 1968 he went on to Clemson, and then Columbia. General Electric in Pleasantville, NY employs him where he serves in Human Resources. He is somewhat like my Dan, born on October 4, 1970 in Tarboro. "Danny" holds a Bachelors degree from UNC-Wilmington and has not the affinity of ancestry like James or I. James has met my half uncle's ex-wife, Mrs. Douglas Townsend from the Mt. Olive area. She is Postmaster at Blowing Rock, North Carolina. Perhaps one day James will take the Townsend Association's sponsored DNA tests, and we might see how we are related in the gene pool of Townsend's tested thus far.

Chapter Fourteen

Poor Records: Obvious and Not So Obvious

Novices working with early history and particularly colonial times are at times surprised and find it difficult working with time, fire, or failure of man to keep records. It seems that unless there was a John White or Artist, or Ship Captain or Clerk recording things, that data simply failed to find its way into early records. This is particularly true in early colonial times.

This is not strange as many did not write or had no need of it in their daily report. Daily life was filled with the challenge of fighting elements of brave and new lands and peoples, void of their own support system. Certainly no records were important when death was a daily encounter.

State Archives are rich if you know what to look for and how to find it. Research on the World Wide Web draws on the Quakers in London and those who have researched the 1620s-40s from strongholds in England or France.

Most Carolinian families find that births were not officially recorded until the 18th century, even though the census of 1790 helps us, especially Robeson County's. Let's examine the genealogical proof like that found in the Bladen County archives, which preceded Robeson County. There we find the 1778 Maxfield Will that mentions some of the persons we like to learn about: Thomas, his wife Leticia, and Richard McConkey. While this is a Bladen County document we can presume it tells a not-so obvious message about the Scottish people who flooded into the town of Kelly on the northern side of the Cape Fear River.

Thomas was no stranger to clashes. He fought in the Spanish Alarm at the time of the Scots movement and was paid, and he undoubtedly fought Indian skirmishes and diseases his whole life. Many good American pioneers we research, fought the Brits in the Separation from the crown, in the founding of his free land in 1782.

The 1790 Census does help clarify who was living with whom, and where. It shows Thomas' family, his wife Leticia and his son William, in the Robeson records. We later census see records that clearly help us in identifying different Townsends in Robeson. The mid-1800 shows Townsends also living then, namely Civil War veteran William Townsend (for whom we had a reunion in 1982) and his father, Alfred. I have visited both gravesites. Alfred's cemetery was in ill repair in 1981 and there were mostly light wood markers when I was there last.

William's will is in Robeson records and further spells out relationships of the period. Many of the conditions of the early times existed simultaneously with events. Mostly trails, rivers and streams, immigrants from Scotland, river and coastal pirates, existed along growth of Kelly and Cross Creek. What is obvious is that without roads, rivers gave Townsends a way to travel to there homes or back to seaports and open seas. Villages north of Little Pee Dee sprang up with Lumbees and migration grew along royal proclamations from James City and Borough of York into precincts in Albemarle County. People of the era moved by water. They moved up and down the colonial coast on rivers just as we prefer roads today. The Settlements of Races by 1776 shows early movement from James Citie down the Chowan River to the Chowan Precinct on the Albemarle Sound, as early as 1685. This is Document in the 1908 Ashe History Map, identifying early North Carolina settlements. This map was available in Hackney Library of Rocky Mount, North Carolina in 1982, but Greensboro Public Libraries no longer has a copy of the aged document.

Chapter Fifteen

Trip to Jamestowne: 400th Celebration of 1607

Trip to Jamestowne: 400th Celebration of 1607

400th Celebration with Queen Elizabeth on hand for events!

May 10th was hot in 2007. We went to Jamestowne to see the three ship replicas. I was not aware that passengers slept on "barrels" with only straw mats to comfort their bones during a voyage to the Canary Islands off Africa. The crossed the south Atlantic to South America across the Antilles past Dominica, Haitian islands, and skirting the southeast coast to James River inlet in Virginae. Each island beginning with the Canary's provided colonial sailors with fresh drinking water, fruit to aid the sorry diet of brick-hard biscuits, dry cereal and seed aboard ship. Nineteen hands were given a gallon of 2% beer each day. It would "keep" at air temperature and not spoil as would water or even fresh meat. Life aboard was sorely cramped, with no latrine provisions.

We also visited replica-Indian villages and saw how Indian corn was grown. I purchased some first-of-a-kind, red corn seed to plant back in Carolina. We visited Jamestown's straw huts, viewed deer and animal skins tanning processes, and observed huge cut trees being burned out, to serve as canoes. As we trekked we visited the original Jamestowne church, which held a "mandatory attendance policy for all colonial citizens, with severe penalties in place for any colonist who did not show up each day at noon".

Also impressive was the governor's home with imported English tile. The presenter was from London and hailed from East Anglia, also home to Townshends there. Her tightly styled red hair, and costume were apropos, English accent and demeanor seemed and quite fitting. We were very curious about the ship replicas moored on the James River, but were forced to leave the cite by security personnel who cleared the area for the President's party, and the crowds had to be moved away from the piers at Jamestowne. This was the 400th Celebration, and dignitaries were on hand, including Britain's Princess, and the President.

The next morn we were shuttled to the Jamestowne dig and were stunned to see the early walls twelve feet below today's surface, after only four hundred years! This was not Egypt, it had not been four thousand years, and why would twelve feet already bury a river settlement? We followed the excavation with interest.

A Marble placard in the original Old Church boasted a memorial to honorable Dr. John Potts, MD. I was not impressed, but rather amused. This 1621-1635 leader was not so important as to care for indentured servant Captain Richard Townsend, who failed to learn Apothecary or Surgery from Potts. Townshend brought his complaint to the Burgesses in the Virginia Company, and the acting burgesses awarded him freedom from Potts, and twenty-one acres of land among Indian lands. This was to be his homestead.

The following day we visited old Williamsburg. The cordwainer~ shoemaker, tannery, and bookshop were personally interesting. The Raleigh Bakery smelled great, and afterwards we spoke with journeymen at the bindery. We visited the cooper, and brick maker. We wanted to purchase the unique triangular postage stamp, but the whole area as well as Carolina seemed to be "out" of stock on this unique postage stamp.

Mrs. Kathy Townsend was badly burned and had sore legs standing in long lines waiting for a burger and freedom fries. Some lines seem to have no beginning or end with about seventy-thousand celebrants reportedly at the 400th Anniversary remembering 1607 in Virgina.

The next day we went to Williamsburg Pottery. Although Kathy and I were excited to meet a descendent of Pocahontas' one Mrs. Griggs from Providence, I endured a day most men would rather forget. A "woman's visit" to the Pottery, I simply sweated it out, as some six hours passed as candles, pitcher, jugs, terra cotta, and flowers were loaded on our carts. I "think" was glad this celebration was more than Jamestowne. It was about my family and love of our lives. In fact, our tales remembering our puppies the following day was delightful.

Little [fourteen pound] Greyson Townsend, a leg lifter, and Sophie-girl were only two years old but had grown to become our "children." They brought us laughter, strange habits, and silly behavior that are appropriate in our home and it was good to be back home in Carolina with them again. We had boarded them in a kennel during our trip to Jamestown, some five or six hours away. We reveled in the memories, thinking about the trip.

Chapter Sixteen

Reviewing what is Known

Through the synapses of e-mail, U.S. mails, passages of time, seemingly endless book clutter, phone calls, manuscripts, interviews and data from Townsend Family Tree DNA recipients, I have found it universal theory that everyone from Kate Townsend Biggs of the 1940-50 era, *The Robesonian,* and then Ms. Ruffin seems to believe the same general theories. Matilda Townsend Ruffin whom I met in 1980 as well as Peggy Townsend in Red Springs, believes that Thomas Townsend represents the end of the line in the search for Townsend family roots. Indeed most of Peggy's early writings to TSA were seemingly there with genealogical keepers like Lewis Townsend, but that was Peggy's book, published in 1970. Yet it seemed shelved, silent, and unrecognized chairmen & genealogists of the Townsend Association when I visited in Oyster Bay during the October-Fall meeting of 2006.

During my historic trek to Oyster Bay I had the opportunity to be the speaker for the meeting. My presentation centered on colonial North Carolina, on the very rare book I brought as gift, Oates's ***History of Fayetteville***, and on my manuscript, *In Search of Thomas.* I was taken with the inquisitive approach by some and the esoteric, genealogical fellows there. Few seemed to really care about quests or ventures. I personally had experienced a high adventure, as had many Townsends in the search for our link to England. I had been to Raynham Hall in England, seen inside, and taken a few photographs. I had held a St Pauls reunion and allowed my research manuscript into Fayetteville's Ray Avenue Public Library--- local history section, for twenty-five years. It seemed to many to be worthy of Townsend family recognition and I secretly wished the TSA had embraced the updated data and findings enthusiastically.

Daniel speaks to TSA in fall of 2007 about
North Carolina history.

Then, oddly, fate came knocking at door. I could no longer work as an instructor of Spanish or History. I experienced strokes, which humbled my take at life and limited my ability to tackle "search" projects. Nevertheless, I fought on. I withdrew the work I had left about twenty-five years previously and began anew to look at possibilities for finding my ancestor, Thomas Townsend.

Unquestionably there would be a few souls "waiting in the wings" to shoot holes in my work. It would seem some folk are prideful and human nature being what it is. I have copied, or mailed every interested party I know or could reach to tell them about upgrades in the work and the changes in the ending. It has been up to each person to share what they know and research has been unveiled. So our results remain conclusive as far as I am able to find and prove, and my research goes on beyond this day although I am quite satisfied with the Jamestown connection theory. Let's back up just a bit.

Thomas Townsend, our chief character was moving, as did many pioneers, with relative Solomon Townsend. It is most likely that they moved with those emigrating Scots. They came by shipload after 1745 up the Cape Fear Basin. Thomas and Solomon were caught up in my most favorite war, the Spanish Alarm of 1747. The ruins at Brunswick towne remains but a hallow shell which is still on the western Cape Fear River buttress where the river turns west from the inlet. A placard has the name of the Topsail Isle Light Infantry from nearby naming who fought there. Thomas was a member of the Topsail Light Infantry. The placard cites this fighting force for collectively protecting settlers from the Spanish attack of the "Loretta" Ship. Infantrymen and colonist were summoned from Campbelton and lands near Flora MacDonald as far away as colonial Anson County. Thomas and Solomon did skirmish and were paid for Spanish Alarm service. This event in Brunswick towne, across from Wilmington was on the Cape Fear River. Both men returned to homesteads and both have wills and properties that are among the Scots in both settlements.

In examining the possible Edisto-Charleston connections for our Thomas Townsend, I looked at James Townsend's work from Rock Hill. He is removed from Anderson---removed from Charleston and Edisto. He claims to be descended from Thomas of Lynn, Massachusetts and hence from England. This as his connection to Townshends. He also found his family connections in a laundry in Charlotte. Yes, I said it correctly. It seems the lady who ran the laundry business was a genealogist! Interestingly, his father was ***not in*** the family tree!

Once in place, he was complete and explicably complete in the family tree. James, of course, has many other wrinkles and stories, which fill in the gaps, but this information, helped me with my own work. James had visited a laundry while in the *Queen City* and talked to a genealogist who happened to be there. They spoke of his family and she knew of his family, but well. It seems she was missing the birth of his father! With that piece in tact, his chart was complete to Lynn, Massachusetts. It was a find of momentous importance. Now, if we could just convince James to complete the TSA swab for DNA results!

I examined a chart by ***ancestry.com*** with Susan Townsend, native of Richmond who married my brother William Frank. Susan had access to several family trees, which originally showed that brother Frank belonged to the 1621 Jamestowne Virginia Townsends. This was enough to give me pause. I wanted to know more about this ***One World Tree*** that kept saying we were from Virginia. I could not shed the findings from Leland Townsend's books, to contact by phone and mail with a Frances (traced roots to Virginia) in Texas, with my research with James Citie and York.

After two years, I contacted *Salt Lake City's ancestry.com* and paid monthly for a relationship with the massive data accumulated at Ancestry.com. They helped me work with One World Tree. This purchased service aid eventually helped me find the roots to Thomas and William and Richard. These were the links I wanted and located some early written records of land ownership, wills, and ship logs in Virgina.

It remained for me to examine how Kent Townsend another DNA Townsend, and TSA member ***had letters from***

Mrs. Richardson in Florida stating Thomas was born in Chowan County, Chowan Precinct south of Jamestown. I contacted all libraries in person, and followed up with U.S. mail and e-mails. For a line that seemingly has no end to find, it was worthy. That is what "William" and his father William proved to be. Perhaps this is why the name 'William' is so very prevalent in Townsend families in the 1700s and 1800s. In my immediate family there are--- William Townsend, William Frank, William Roscoe, and another William Frank, just to mention those since the civil war. William is a well-revered family name among Townsends

Richard, born in 1601 in County Norfolk, had a second son William, who like all youth wanted a new opportunity and a new life/wife in a new land. Virginia was the place and 1607-10 had been a success after the Lost Colony of 1588 had suffered with no supplies and reinforcements, and settlers left Fort Raleigh. Our Richard came to Virginia per ship logs in about 1620. He owned land and eventually had eldest son, Captain Robert, daughter Frances, and another son William. William had a son named William, as did Robert. Robert's William (whose son was William) was our Thomas father, who moved his lot to Carolina about 1712. And Thomas was born there in the Chowan Precinct about 1725.

I had speculated twenty-five years ago that "Virginia, Edisto Island or Charleston" held equal possibilities for being the home of our Thomas. I knew that the Little Pee Dee became the Lumber River at the border of South Carolina. The River was used to bring logs by Lumbees and settlers alike, the port at George Towne was important and was an early clue to the reason Thomas would have been attracted to Robeson County in the days that rivers were important.

Equally important was the Borough of York on the open Atlantic. It was a few miles closer than the James Towne, and was protected by river barriers and land projections separating it from York or the Atlantic Ocean.

Many family developments and colonial situations that embraced the New World have been lost in the vernacular and mixed brogues and time. The era was a Colonial period of Kings; the land, whether Virginia or Carolina, became all the same. Carolina was further south. Both colonies, like Plymouth Colony far to the North in 1620, were lands of Indian cultures that lived and only they had mastered living in what became the New World to Europeans, our America. Indians were forced from their habitat, as a matter of course. It was not an impressive picture.

In the New World, Europeans lived near water. They moved and traveled by streams and swamps. Here there were no roads except for some hazardous Indian trails, so they ventured only in groups a few miles from Virginia company precinct, and by water. That was, the counties in northeastern Carolina that the King blessed for colonizing, including Chowan Precinct, popular in Black beard reports around 1713.

Almost all had an Indian influence because they were here when the colonists and Richard Townsend came from England as indentured servant in Jamestowne. Thus the immigration to the new world was brave and new. It was courageous and speculative. One gasps at the deathly trip for the likes of women or children, and for those who expected a better life. It was scarcely a better home for those who came first. Hope abounds only for the soulful few with faith and patience: moreover, it abounds most often only in retrospect. We look back to see our Thomas and his father William, and great-grandfather Richard. Each was just like us, only perhaps more resilient and more desperate.

Chapter Seventeen

Chowan, About those Indians,

Tuscarora, Military History

Chowan is not about Murfreesboro or a college by that name. It is believed by a knowledgeable few to be the site of the birthplace of Thomas. It certainly was the jumping off stage for early pioneers who ventured from York, Jamestown by English Kings decree into Carolina. It was home of the flow of travelers who sought new lands, new opportunity and better homes. Many flourished in the 1630s as peoples moved from initial colonial footholds into Virginian Precincts and lands as far south as present day New Bern.

According to records in Chowan County, genealogical research done is extensive. It focuses on settlements from colonist resettling. Of course it adds credibility to the Thomas Townsend birthplace question especially when Robeson County is quite a distance away. It makes sense that he may have been born in North Carolina rather than in York, James Citie area with William, his father, and is part of the movement of peoples or exploration of new lands south of Virginiae.

York and James Citie were open to the ocean and subject to nor'easters, hurricanes, and had no buffers to the elements, as did Jamestown. It was a great Atlantic fishing town but Chowan County was a planned venture that was endorsed by the Crown. So it only makes sense that Capt Robert Townsend or William Townsend's sons, both called "William" Townsend, and their brides would follow folk exploring the trails south and along the way. They gave birth to one Thomas Townsend in 1725. This child became the principal character in this document and led the search for Thomas, circa 1725.

One member of the TSA with Mississippi roots and Thomas foundations supports this belief today and he has been further contacted by email regarding this matter.

About Those Indians

In High Point, NC, in 2006 James Lowry was sixty-two years of age and so was the author of this book. We lived in the same community and attended Covenant Methodist Church. As we compared facts about the Lumber River floating lumber to Georgetown, and how Lumbee Indians taught many new settlers to navigate its stream north of the little Pee Dee. We spoke of Robeson, and of famous Lumbee authors of that area. We spoke of books ***To Die Game*** and ***The Only Land I Know***, which features authors who have conducted, detailed research into Lowries and Thomas' time. Their era was the Bladen County after Albemarle and with the unloading of other Scots, the McConkeys. Lowry's ancestors in Robeson knew the Townsends well. He gave fresh air to my story.

Lumbee Henry Lowry was said to have hidden the Townsend goods, cattle, and hogs along with everything else of value from Sherman's troops. Sherman's *Bluebellies* as the johnny-rebs called them were relentless in their Civil War march and rode upon Lowry and gang much to their chagrin. *Yanks* were slaughtered, maimed and hung upside-down in trees for blue-uniformed, Union troops who followed to see. The invaders didn't face another Lowry on this day, nor William Townsend's family. Dad, Charles Townsend, William and his wife's family found safe harbor on a small island in the Lumber River protected by the Lowry's. They were invited guests of sorts by the Lowries, and Sherman and his marauders made a side-step towards the coast, before a northern march to the Arsenal at Campbelton—La Fayette.

York, Virginia Settlement in 1630 Charles River Shire was one of the eight shires in the dominion and in it was the borough of Yorktowne on the Atlantic. One of the ventures of the crown was the land of the first expedition into Carolina. The Albemarle County had a **Shaftsbury Precinct** to the south towards Queen Anne's creek, later all were renamed. But at the time many settlers were ready for fresh land, then repack and move to new, free lands in outlying precincts such as Shaftsbury. Today we call these North Carolina, and by County name, Chowan, which like many early settlement names were named after *Indian settlements.*

Tuscarora role in the Spanish Alarm

Thomas Townsend was first introduced at the ripe age of twenty-six to the Spanish Alarm along near today's New Hanover. Over one hundred ships from Scotland were landing seeking tax relief, and a new beginning. Taking up with Scots as they settled in and around the great Cape Fear River, he and ally Solomon Townsend were caught up ships of prey that intruded in the perilous waters off Cape Fear at the Atlantic Ocean.

Two Spanish warships ships sailed eighteen miles up the river to a jut of land called Brunswick Town, an English town experiment. This colonial settlement had little room for Parsons or people who would not work. Women and children had to hoe in the fields and work twelve-hour days. The settlement was laid out in squares like a planned township. At any rate, the Spanish Pirates had grown weary of attacking ships that void of precious gold.

The Spaniards decided to attack the town and the ships dropped anchor for the siege. For several days they pounded the settlement in a mosquito-infested area and called to assist the settlers. Members of the called-up infantry were Solomon of Anson County, part of the Scottish movement southwest of Pleasant Hill near Flora MacDonald's land, and our Thomas.

They were fighting the pirates of Spain in an incursion. They were of the Topsail Light group that fired back at Spaniards who mounted boats to come ashore. Some made it; there was fighting all the way.

As the story goes the Spanish during the siege had their way with the colonists, killing settlers, drinking, and eating their food and some unnamed horrors of the debacle.

Left to their own devices the settlers ran into the thickets. In time they ran smack into Tuscarora who didn't like whites to begin with. Already, they had raided and killed many white men. They hated the expansion that took freedom from their waters, and hunting grounds. To emphasize their hatred, and skinned a few settlers and strung them along the trading paths. This violent contact quickly changed the mind of fleeing colonist. Settlers ran back towards their settlement, which was upon their arrival was on fire and in some ruin. The highlight of this report is to clearly say the settlers had on second thought rather fight the marauders, than deal with Tuscarora Indians.

At the end, Thomas, Solomon and Topsail groups gained the upper hand in guerilla techniques, and one drunken Spanish sailor fell into the gunpowder magazine, blowing apart the good ship *Loretta* in the river. The remaining Spanish ship immediately set sail for the Cape Fear River mouth in the Atlantic. The Spaniards remaining from the sinking Loretta swam or floated ashore to become slaves for life. Such was that encounter of twin military fronts for Townsends.

Military History of the Townsends

Next on the colonial horizon was the Revolutionary War. Many Scots in Carolina had sworn allegiance to the King after the Scottish defeat at Culloden. The risk-taking pioneers were settlers facing death from the plights of long dangerous journeys to a New World. Finding tax relief of ten years, granted by the King, they came to Cape Fear by the thousands in 1746. They were the Tories, not in favor of the warring colonists who wished no taxes without local representation.

Thomas was among those who served his land and lot by working in the war to fight the English during two-plus years of the War between colonist and mother England. He was a deserving representative for our family to look backwards and recognize as founding father.

His final home secures the touchstone of this environment near Fayetteville, today the site of Fort Bragg, the largest military base in the world.

William Townsend of Robeson County, to whom much is owed, was a sharpshooter in the Civil War. My great grandfather was recent enough for my own dad, D. V.

Townsend, Sr, to tell me stories about him. For example, William was to have been asked by wife Ora, "William, I think I'd like a piece of cheese." To which he replied, "Yes Ma'am", and William would walk two miles to town to get that cheese for his wife!

William was a tall, thin gent. He was about 6'6", wife Ora at five feet tall, was full-blooded French from a long line of French blood. Ora's genes may have affected her offspring's height. D. V. and his children were all about 5'9" or 5'10". My sons are above 6'0" and DVT, III is 6'2".

William was in the North Carolina Infantry and during its glory days the southern troops were well equipped and well fed. Assigned to the Northern Virginia front as Marksman, William was said to have shot across a crevasse, clearing for General Lee pointing to the Northern positions. This was to have been tremendously helpful in an era when hand-to-hand fighting was a deadly encounter much like legendary William Wallace of Scotland's fighting fame.

In the years following, William marched in Civil War memorial parades that were famous, large, important, prideful and most times hot. I believe Confederate Memorial Day is a summer event and it can be unbearably hot, walking in parades.

Those attending our 1982 Reunion remarked mostly how hot the parades were. The old soldiers were proudly wearing their soldier pins, rifles, and marching with horses, wagons, and of course, dust.

William is buried with his pin still on his vest. His old rustic Civil War Iron Cross taken by Lon Townsend and placed in Jean T. Duncan's garage for safekeeping has eluded me. I reported that it went missing and but no sheriff or family member seemed willing to locate the relic or seek its whereabouts. Trying to join the Sons of Confederacy, I learned that the Lumberton Camp would replace his Civil War Cross but I have not heard from them in the past three months.

During World War II, Dad or D.V. was a Medical Corpsman at Fort Bragg and lived at Sullivan Boarding House responsible for the bars, prostitutes, and soldier fights that frequented in the infamous fifth block of downtown Fayetteville. Also, Dad was a welder at the shipyards in Wilmington. Having a wife with child, he wasn't asking to serve overseas, but he was willing to serve. The Townsend men have always seemed willing.

I came along during the Viet Nam conflict. I completed Army ROTC at Wake Forest but failed the physical exam. I appealed to the Surgeon General but was denied admission to the Army. As it turned out, many good friends in high school and college died in Viet Nam. So I may have been fortunate. Football knees injuries and old boating mishaps kept me from meeting stringent Army requirements.

Although I was draft board classified 1-Y during Viet Nam, many soldiers left this land in honor and glory. No matter the war. In American history they are the Colonial Independence war, the French and Indian, the Civil War, Spanish, World Wars, Korea, Nam, and Iraq. In each there were soldiers who faced early death, mangled limbs, pain, suffering, anguish, and loss of will. Many had psychological damage, depression, despair and self-loathing, which crippled soldiers returning to wives, family and neighbors. These broken people had uphill struggles, though Fort Bragg today says only 1% quitters face court martials in time of war, thousands despairingly quit and come home. The after-glow of heroic battles is married by such despair.

Chapter Eighteen

Early Theories & Ideas About Thomas' Roots

It seems that many peoples have subscribed to concepts of their branch of the tree. One Ellee Townsend of Lumberton attended the St Paul's family reunion in 1982 and wrote me in October of that year. She cited the three Townsend brothers from England, Richard, Henry and John. She said her father was descended from John. John had settled in a town called Raynham, one in Back Swamp and one in Southern-most North Carolina.

Reverend Odom has referred to a book, *Kinfolk*, that is in the Lumberton library and Ms Dudley Jennings was the contact to reference material. Interestingly this sounds like *Harlee's Kinfolks* that Matilda spoke of in contacts with her work, which researched genealogy paid for by depression-era funds. These were a part of W.P.A project of FDR in 1933.

Ellee went on to write that her dad had always been told that he was descended from John. My grandfather's brothers where Charles, William who had issue: Sandie, Lawrence or *Lonnie*, Reverend Berter, and my grandfather, William Frank. We of course recognize Berter as the home of my orphaned-at-twelve father, D.V., and William Frank as his dad, and my grandfather.

Circa 1992 Kent Townsend says that he received U.S. mail from Mrs. Richard Daniel Robinson in Florida. They have that data or research. Mrs. Robinson shows a Henry Townsend married to Ann Bacon, who had Roger. Roger married to Anne died about 1621. The couple had Richard. Richard born about 1611 married Hannah and they had William. (They also had issue Thomas, Joseph, John, Mary, and a Richard.)

William in South Carolina had sons. One was Thomas. William died about 1730. Mrs. Robinson examined wills in South Carolina determining Thomas' father was this William. Thomas was referred to in the will of a relative as the son of William. That is a curious twist to our efforts since no one has ever mentioned their names before. Of course in Grinds Wills we previously heard that Thomas was referred to as the son of William, but not in this particular context.

In letters and books from Leland and Peggy the information about Richard as indentured servant to James City, Virginia was plentiful. There were comments about his fighting for his freedom. Captain Richard Townsend was judged not to have received his requisite tutorials under his by Dr. Potts. That is the positive purpose of an indentured servant. In fact, he subsequently was able to win his freedom from indenture due to the failure of Potts to develop his skills or knowledge. His steadfast posture in James Citie proved him worthy and York County Library's Anne Colton provided records of his early land holdings about the Indian lands. His grandson was William, and while only an esoteric few hold to the theory of Thomas' origin here, Mrs. Robinson of the prior passage in her letters to Kent did say that Thomas was born in Chowan County. Chowan was a precinct of Virginiae Company and not a North Carolina area as such. It was an English King's charter Albemarle County. Native Indians and Virginians freely moved south from James City and York Towne to find new pioneer, colonial homes. Most frequently families moved to homestead in neighboring shires, which were later known to be Carolina. At this stage little was known of Carolina, as the 1588 colony at Roanoke Island had been "lost". So it was near the Chowan River, just south of today's Norfolk, Virginia, which was named after County Norfolk, England.

Some believe his line to be of "Thomas of Lynn" family Townshend. James Townsend of Blowing Rock is formerly from Anderson, family beforehand removed from Fenwick Hall, Charleston, and Edisto Island, South Carolina. Peggy Townsend and I have been beleaguered with hopes that James or Daniel his son will join the Townsend Society's DNA research of the TSA to help prove our line to Raynham via Thomas of Lynn. This would be momentous for us all!

We have stalled on the idea of Daniel Townsend as possible father or grandfather to our "Thomas". This Daniel Townsend was apparently born to Thomas of Lynn, Massachusetts and relocated to Charleston. He was thirty when arriving in

1688. So the question of his age is an issue when we think of our Thomas' age. This question arose when Kate Townsend Biggs suggested Daniel of Edisto Island might have fathered "Thomas". Early in 1980 there were research questions about this "Daniels" age to young to allow him to "father", at age twelve, was it even possible? Or perhaps his son? Both seemed unlikely or impossible based on age calculations at that time.

Perhaps Daniel of Edisto had an *illegitimate son* who immigrated into North Carolina from the Pee Dee River Basin or Charleston. These things we may only speculate.

We do know that James in the paragraph above found part of his family line on a rare trip to a Charlotte laundry. The lady running the laundry, who was also a genealogist, had his whole family, except his father. He knew who he was. James' family tree minus his son Dan, James, and his father. Once included, the family tree was complete.

Chapter Nineteen

Family Evolution after 1980

James Townsend of Blowing Rock and Rock Hill may yet help us find another key to Thomas Townsend's origin, unless

Alfred Townsend from a Ten-Type, 1819

you are now ready to accept Jamestowne, Virginia 1621 as the birthplace of our family Townsend, Thomas' family tree.

Richard Townshend of County Norfolk, United Kingdom came to *Virginiae* as indentured servant to Dr. Robert Potts,

MD. Potts, a London speculator, was willing to depart in 1621 with Townshend and bring Apocary-surgery to Virginiae Company at Jamestowne. On a ship called Abigail following the good ship George; they arrived James Citie in 1620. Townsend using Virginiae Company charter demands freedom though the Virginiae Company. They had only judicial burgesses of sorts, no courts [Richard Townsend was later to serve on Colonial House of Burgess for years]. The Virginiae Company *burgesses* awarding him 21 acres of Indian lands and his freedom from Potts in 1621. Potts is memorialized today in the Jamestown Anglican Church with a large marble stone in the wall, carved to recognize his tenure there until 1635.

Richard married Frances Baldwin in 1639. His third child was William born in 1644(d.9.19.1675), who married Sarah Churchill, daughter of Henry. Captain Robert, his first was born in 1640, and married Mary Longhorne. Captain Robert and Mary Longhorne had several girls, the first married in 1692. Robert Baldwin was third born to the union, and then William was born as their fourth child. William, born about 1674.

This William and his wife made trips into Shaftsbury precinct, and later Chowan precinct in North Carolina. It was there Thomas was born in 1725. Thomas moved slowly over northeast, and downward with Virginians such as the

Affords, Thompsons, and other former Virginia Company families into present-day North Carolina. New settlements and lands began to open. By 1747, the Scots were unloading hundreds of ships at the Cape Feare Basin, after the Battle of Culloden, in Scotland. Over 150 ships came to in Kelly, Elizabethtown, and Cross Creek. Among these settlers were many single lassies.

Letisha McConkey and another Scotch woman soon to be Solomon Townsend's wife. Ships unloaded daily. Thomas was smitten by Robert McConkeys daughter, Lettice, and soon took this faire Scottish lassie for his bride. They homesteaded in Bladen land, soon to be named Robeson.

Thomas' second-born was William, born on 4/16/1750 and married on 8/28/1783 to Sarah Thompson. William died 2/12/1839. William was a strong man as was his strong colonial wife Sarah. Their tombstones caused quite a stir in 1982 when they were moved from existing gravesites on Lumberton's Country Club to Asbury Church in Raynham, NC.

William's fifth of nine children was Charles. Charles was born 4/16/1792; married to Martha B. Humphrey in 1815, and he died 11/1/1865. His lightwood gravesite is at Odom Cemetery in Robeson where he lived. The second-born of fourteen children was Alfred.

Alfred Townsend, married Edith Humphrey and Margaret Britt. The second wife was Peggy Townsend's namesake. This image about 1819. His bearded photo was a present to me 1982 from Peggy. It was a *tintype* photo and he appears to be about sixty-five, unshaven which may well have been the style, a farmer, with physical characteristics that makes old photos helpful. Alfred had two wives and twelve children, a list of names and dates are available.

The second wife lived into the 20th century when her namesake was born one Margaret Tyner who married to John Townsend. This is the Peggy Townsend of Buie of whom I have spoken earlier in this book. Peggy provides 1970 data that melds with Ruffin-Biggs Townsend

Alfred's son William was a Southern gentleman I hold in high esteem. William born April 2, 1842 he married *Sis Arrey* as many called her, or Orrie Prevatte who was born on 9/4/1847. A Civil War veteran, my own father was reared on his farm home near Parkton. Dad said Grandpa William had a unique way of stirring new potatoes on the porch, of the Robeson home place. He would use a tomato stick and stir the new potatoes in a bucket of water, removing all the tender skins. Readers, I have tried this technique, and it works! William told my father many tales that have been passed down, one generation to another. One concerned the authority to behead murderers, high thieves and criminals in old England.

Orrie, William's wife is the French woman whose genes may have resulted in lowering our family height. "Prevatte" is an old Robeson family name and is still at this printing, prolific in Eastern Carolina. William and Orrie had issue: James Alexander (Sandy Townsend born 1/1/1867; Callie M, born 6/13/68,Ellen born 5/18/70; Lonnie H. born 10/25/73; Berder born 6/21/76 and William Franklin born 11/21/1882.

Civil War William's son William "Frank" Townsend was 7" shorter than his dad. His mother, Ora, was 5' foot even, and may have stunted Townsend men for 3 generations. Frank lived with his dad and grandfather in near Parkton. His neighbor was Judge Lycurgus Varser of Lumberton. Frank's first wife, who did prematurely, was Robeson's loveliest Flora Ausley. His second wife fell ill with pneumonia. She was my grandmother Mamie Rich Carter, and thirdly, Inez Wells of Pender County who was there when William, Orrie, and her husband William Frank age 53, died. Each of his three wives bore him children: Mildred; D.V., Beulah, William Roscoe; and---Douglas and Claude.

Daniel Varser, Sr. was born on May 5, 1918 in Vander, home **of** my grandmother Carter, not the William Frank's Robeson home. D.V. was oldest of three. He had four children, of which I was the third child, Daniel Varser. Jr, born on March 16, 1944 in Fayetteville.

D.V. or dad had married Alma L. Sullivan in Dillon, South Carolina in 1938. Also born into this union were Mamie Patricia in 1940, James Daniel who died of SIDS in 1942; and my brother William Frank who was born on a warm Spring May 10, 1953.

After completing college and my Personnel career was launched, I married Mary Ellen Dehmer on September 28, 1969 at St. Patrick's Catholic in Fayetteville. I was twenty-six and Mary was twenty-one. We had four children as I go to press with this book: Daniel Varser, III, was born in 1970; Jennifer Lynn, born in 1972, Michael Bradford, born in 1975; and Robert Matthew born in 1977. Currently there are no male Townsend's to take this family line further. Perhaps

Douglas Townsend Jr in Charlotte has a male grandson? Perhaps Michael, Robert, or even Daniel will bring a male child into the world of Townsends.

Chapter Twenty

Townsend Family Evolution after 1980

Some readers who seek only genealogical answers about Thomas Townsend may feel disappointed that I have chosen to report the Townsends of the 20th and 21'st century. For me, this altruistic quest became a story not only of who we were, but also who we became. So I have used biographical data to log the family that may prove of interest in coming ages. Today it may be just information, but in time it may prove to tie Townsends to their heritage. I don't want you to lose your focus of interest in Thomas, but the whole story is about our search for Thomas and becoming aware of when Townsend had become.

Certainly the DNA tests to which Daniel Earle and I belong along with Peggy, George, but especially an Irish minister is noteworthy. D. Earle and I have collaborated several times over matters and he sent me information regarding his trip to Castle Townshend in Ireland. Here is what he said.

Several Townsends have been making references to the Townshends in Ireland. Last October my wife and I spent two nights at a bed and breakfast on the south coast of Ireland in the village of Castletownshend. The B&B is located in a castle from which the village takes its name. The owner Anne Cochrane-

Townshend is direct descendant of Colonial Richard who came from England to Ireland with the army of Oliver Cromwell in the mid 1600s.

My wife has Irish and Scotch-Irish ancestors so we hoped to find some links during our visit. When I had the DNA results from the Long Island Townsend Association I was surprised to see not only was I related to William Townsend (1750-1830) of Robeson County.

Also, a Reverend Edward G. H. Townshend of England, whose ancestors for many generations had lived in Ireland, came to Ireland with Oliver Cromwell!

Since returning from the trip we verified that Reverend Edward Townsend is indeed a descendant of Colonial Richard is therefore a distant cousin of my B&B host back in Castletownshend. It is clear that per the DNA I am also a distant cousin with Reverend Edward Townsend who now is up in years and suffers Parkinson's.

20th Century: Mixture of Lines

Jim Sullivan at 20. The Jernigan-Sullivan name is one from Ireland, and after the potato blight of about 1850, as Alma Louise Sullivan (Townsend) recalls, the Sullivans made their way to Carolina like many Scotch-Irish before them. John Henry,

James Hubert, James Alexander; all these men often developed heart trouble. Looking in the family years back I had spoken to a Mr. Black in Burlington, the home of Sullivan roots in Carolina. He traced the Sullivans as well a "Susan" from Fayetteville.

Needless to say, Alma Louise, my mother, was sibling to Virginia Sullivan Wilson of Lumberton and her issues Coble D. Jr and Mary Louise. Jim Sullivan and wife gave birth to James who had a daughter, and Harry who left a son Steve in Long Island as a mechanic, a son Harry, Jr or "Rocky" in Florida, and Mike in New York also.

Son Bill was killed accidentally at age eighteen, in own garage, as the result of an electrical accident. Peggy, Harry's wife and mother of four boys, is remarried. She moved to California. Of course there was George Click, foster son---a calm spirits who smiled often and his presences conjured up the feelings of hope, charity, and love itself. He was killed in his sailor whites; hitch hiking to Quantico in 1953 when a car flipped as the driver fell asleep.

One Carl Chandler was best friend to my Uncle James Sullivan. Court in that town held Chandler accountable for James's death at Chandler's home on Morganton Road. Incidentally, Mother always said I was most like her brother James. My own brother, Frank lived on the Chandler home site after major residential rebuilding took place years later at Morganton Arms and Woodrow Streets.

Let's look at others in my family. The Carter name is an English name. The Carters were prolific as a family and Mamie Rich was the first of fifteen children born to Docia and Big Dan Carter. Mamie Rich Carter, pictured above is Big Dan to left and Docia Carter to right. Mamie Carter is pictured at a young 18. Both parents were "Carters" and so she was considered "Carter" mixed by two bloodlines. The author recalls Carter reunions where TV-repairman Paul,

Lester, Jr.-attorney, friend and Judge, and Derb the Judge would corner DV and embrace him. I was always proud they accepted us, and seemed so happy we came. We were always recognized and warmly welcomed even though their Mamie Rich had married William Frank *Townsend* and died at such an early age about 1930.

She was a wonderful woman according to her brother, Charles P. Carter. Charles provided Alma and DV the auto to go to Dillon to marry in South Carolina, as Alma was not of age to marry in North Carolina. I interviewed Grandmother Mamie's youngest brother, Charles Carter of Carolina Beach. Using a cassette tape, I asked questions about Mamie Carter, and her son William Roscoe. He was helpful in my gathering of vintage Carter facts about the departed. I learned much which I have recorded in this book elsewhere.

I met and visited Grandmother's brother, King Wilson Carter who grew peanuts at the Carter home place near Macedonia Church. It had a separate, breezeway attached room for cooking and was and the country home was elegant sharing history of earlier eras. It was home to Big Dan and Docia Carter. It was striking and memorial to the fifteen children who were born there.

William Roscoe Townsend, Dad's brother, was taken to Vander in Cumberland County after William Frank's death at age fifty-three. He lived with them until he suddenly drowned the last day of school. He ran ahead of his classmates, and

Lester Carter believes he was too tired from the run when he hit the cold, spring-fed Bullard Mill Pond that May first. He was playing with schoolmates including interviewed girl friend, Gaynele Beard.

Lester Carter was a practicing attorney for fifty years and recently sent me clippings about his career. He is now eighty years old. His brother Buck grows strawberries in Vander. He is very successful and both senior citizens have survived to help tell about Carters today.

Townsend: 1969 The Dehmer's, a Germanic heritage

Mary Ellen Dehmer was born in New York, in Flushing, Queens, on March 21 1949. She married Daniel V. Townsend, Jr in St. Patrick's Catholic Church on September 27, 1969. This was the church near the Dehmer home on Purdue in Briarwood Estates, Fayetteville, where Mary had graduated high school and was a student and secretary at technical college and Black Decker Plant, where Daniel worked. Mary had siblings: Paul A., Allen, Margaret, and Chris.

Their mother Mary Lou was from South Bend, and Paul A. was a New York-born Notre Dame graduate. The Dehmer's, a second-generation German family, were close to grandparents who visited from Flushing and all the men were electro-mechanically gifted. Also, they were knowledgeable of building and skilled at all things technical of the age. The Dehmer's moved to Charleston to favor the warmer ocean climate, and after Captain Dehmer's retirement from the United States Air Force. Paul's parents who were products of Ellis Island emigration and high risers, who had lived in New York.

German know-how was the hallmark as Paul the eldest was a master and built a Boeing career in Kent, Washington with Boeing and his wife Sandy formerly from Hickory, North Carolina. Alan and Beth (of New Hampshire) are historians, and photographers in Durham today. Margaret works in Colorado; Chris recently married in Atlanta, is a national project manager. The Dehmer family thrives whether on vacation, or at work living in this era.

Chapter Twenty-One

Broken Limbs and Twisted Twigs

James Townsend seems to be a link to Thomas of Lynn by way of Daniel of Edisto, South Carolina. James has given of himself to complete the Townsend Family DNA that could pave the way for the Thomas of 1725 to be of his line.

If that is true, it will undoubtedly change the mindset of Ancestry.com and others who believe settlers in Yorktowne and Jamestowne marshaled us to the American continent circa 1607-1621. I planned and attended the 400th anniversary of Jamestowne, Virginia.

***Danny and Michelle are pictured
shortly after marriage in 2007***

Daniel V. Townsend, III. or Danny, was born to Mary Dehmer Townsend and Daniel Jr on October.4, 1970, in Tarboro where Dan was Personnel Manager for a new Black and Decker Plant. Danny was born about midnight after a beautiful Sunday, and Mary's 9 1/2-month pregnancy was over. A joy had begun. Danny carried the Townsend line a step further. He married April Michelle in Greensboro on June 22,2007.

Danny adds "Michelle's three children from a previous marriage are fun for us as family, Nathan Ryan, and Stephen Kyle were born March.2, 19.98 and Courtney on March 7, 19.95." Danny had been third of our four children to marry. His birth and marriage helped the possibility of growing the Thomas Townsend line forward from 1725 as more Townsend children were planned.

Pictured are Jennifer, Art, and Son Mason in Colorado

Second born to the author was Jennifer Lynn Townsend-Larkin born December 11, 1972 Baltimore. She was born on her paternal grandmother's birthday! Having earned degrees with UNC, University of Denver, and Colorado Graduate Business School. She and husband Art Larkin a Colorado *pioneer*, works Sun Micro Systems as an Engineer in Westminster, Colorado, where they live. Jenn was transferred from UNC Chili's to Denver where she met Art more than a decade ago. Now they have son Mason Patrick in tow.

They work as professionals at Sun Micro Systems. Here is Art's lineage. Arthur Patrick was born April 7,1966 in Denver. Arthur George Larkin Sr his dad was born June 1, 1909 in Council Bluff Iowa, and died Oct 4, 1975. His wife, Elna Fern Dressler was born July of 1910 in Atlanta, Kansas, and died December 23, 1950.

Art's mother Carol Ann Williams-Larkin was born December 24, 1938 in Denver. Her dad was Reginald George Williams born on June 24, 1908 in Russell Gulch, CO and died on August 18, 1951. His wife, Ester Mae Unruh-Williams was born on July 2, 1902 in Enid, OK and died on March 29, 1951. This is the heritage of the Arthur's roots out west. As indicated, he is a *pioneer!*

In reviewing lineage—which includes Jennifer's mother, I find that the Dehmer's have a Germanic heritage tied to Catholicism and tradition. Paul Allen Dehmer, Mary Ellyn Dehmer-Townsend's father was born in Queens, New York on March 20,1924. His father was Germanic, Paul A Dehmer born on January 17, 1895 who married Augusta Albert-Dehmer of Brooklyn.

My best deciphering is that his grandfather was Domiukus Hobenzoldarn, who was born on November 6, 1883 married to Anna Eakert of Bavaria, Germany on November 14, 1860. His Grandmother's parents were Joseph Albert born on May 13, 1861 and wife Elisabeth Storch Albert.

Mary Lou Dehmer, Mary's mother was a South bend, Indiana native-born, Burkhart on November 25, 1924. Her father was Anselm Burkhart born in Ontario on February 28, 1876. He was married to Helen Janowski who was born South Bend on July 31, 1898. The Burkhart line goes back to Anselm Badden Baden, Germany. One wife, Bridget Doyle, was of County Clair, Ireland. The grandparents of Mary Lou are Polish. Namely, Michael Janowski born in Poznan, Poland in 1852 and Josephine Kukupa also born in Poznan, Poland, in 1856.

Mary Lou or Grandmother Dehmer provides this data regarding her mother's side of her family. Mary Lou Dehmer's mother was Helen Janowski born on July 31, 1898 and died on August 6, 1968. Helen's mother was Josephine Kalupa and grandfather was Michael Janowski born October 19, 1852, died in November on the 3, 1973. Anne Kolupa was Grandmother's Dehmer's mother, and she was married to Michael Kalupa.

Similarly, grandfather's mother was Cordelia and her husband was Michael. Grandmother Mary Lou Dehmer in closing said,

"My siblings were Matthew 1879-1939; Vernon 1879-1936; Joanne 1886-1906; Stella 1884--; Katie1891-1961; and Alexander."

Michael Bradford Townsend, 3rd child born to Mary Dehmer and Daniel V. Townsend, Jr married Leah Cauley of Kinston at a lovely wedding at the Episcopal Church at UNC in Chapel Hill, North Carolina. Leah has a Master's in Accountancy from UNC, and is a CPA, while Mike completed his PhD at University of Colorado, Boulder. He is Research Biologist with CDC Atlanta.

Pictured are Michael and Leah.

Born August 17, 1977 in Winston-Salem like his older brother Mike, <u>Rob</u>ert Matthew Townsend moved to Wilmington after education in Rocky Mount Schools. After Cape Fear Technical Institute, he worked in food service & Grocery, and Reality. His young daughter Lera and he live with Lera's mom, Holly Claire Howard there today. Here is a 2007 photo of Rob.

Pictured from left to right be sister Jennifer Lynn Townsend-Larkin,

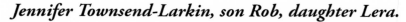

Jennifer Townsend-Larkin, son Rob, daughter Lera.

Afterwards

As the sun goes down on this book, which is for me of some historic achievement, several subjects seem untouchable, yet mentionable. First, *soma types* or body types. I note that upon arrival in America, the Townshends were English bluebloods and upon shipboard starvation and meager diets the first Townsends where likely razor thin as most settlers who perished from starvation, disease, and who were ravaged by malnutrition. As generations grew, influx of races mixed for our family. The Scotch in 1747 with McConkeys, the French with Prevatte's in 1850, Irish in 1890s, the Cherokee in 1900s, and well to do English, planters---the Carters in 1910.

The flavor of the post 1950 era produced paunch comfortable gents who were likely to have said, "*Yes mam', pass the potatoes, I think I'll have a second helping*". The Townsend midriff spread was not always present until about age fifty, but shortly after it emerged like the garden each year to catch the finest families dieting and confounded. What happened to our youthful physiques? Like so many in America as the 21st century it is only a few Townsend's that maintain the physique, but some do. Credit given to those Townsends, who do manage.

Issues of Health

I thank God for our blessings. Also *Alma and D.V.*, my parents for standing with me during my lifetime. After asthma and constant childhood hospitalizations, Mother and I spent many winters at the Carolina coast so I could breathe the salty air and help my airways. I was ill for as early as I recall, my earliest childhood memories were in a cold oxygen tent. It was isolated. After age twelve, I began to outgrow the allergies and asthma. After years of visits to doctors, weekly shots, and expensive care I believed I had arrived, the day dad drove me to little league football tryouts for the Jaycees football.

Afterwards, I went on to play football well in Junior High and High school earning All-America, Most Athletic, Most-Valuable Athlete, and East-West All-Star Honors in 1962. These were achievements for our family, and mother and dad reveled. With one exception. Dad and I attended Duke football for eight years, I then did the unthinkable and accepted a football grant to Wake Forest. Dad's heart sank, but he later recovered. Wake Forest had a disciplined role in life like no other. I remain a loyal Deacon even to this day.

Ugly Twist of Child Bearing

As I studied the number of children each generation brought in issue, I was struck with an observation. The modern experiences have not been so good. For example, my grandfather Frank had three wives, Flora, Mamie, and Inez. While all three had offspring of the Townsend line, Frank died in 1930 when dad was only twelve. The splintered children were never together and family had no rhyme or reason, until 1982. That is fifty -two years later when I began this inquiry. That allows for lots of slippage, poor record keeping, and deaths without notations in many places and counties. Also, Frank's first born, by marriage number two, was my father. He, Daniel Varser had four children, and one might guess the line would easily expand beyond his birth. His first born, Mamie Patricia, his second James Daniel died of Sudden Crib Death, his third born was sick, me. Chances were diminishing all this in the early 1940s that the line could go further. Then the surprise of 1950s, brother Frank was born. Frank suffered a football injury and could not bear children. See what I mean? How would the line go forth? No matter what, chances were slim.

My first-born was Daniel V. III didn't marry until he was 37.5. He married Michelle a fine lady with three children, June 22,2007; my second born was Jennifer Lynn, she married Art and had son. They live in Colorado, but she cannot produce a family line. My third born was Michael Bradford, who married Leah, and they live in Atlanta. They have had no children during the first years. My fourth child Robert Matthew and Holly, and had Lera. Currently with four children there is no male heir to take the Townsend bloodline further.

We now only began to look to Thomas, William, to Robert, and Richard. Will their line end here for family Townsend to move a generation ahead?

Currently, there is one possibility, Inez, William. Frank Townsend's third wife before he died at age 53 bore two sons. Douglas, who became a Police Chief in Blowing Rock, had a son in Charlotte. Perhaps he will have children that will extend the family there, from St Pauls onward.

Lastly let me confess my gratitude. If I were living in another country or era, I would not be alive today to finish this work for my progeny. I had a massive stroke in 2005 after I completed teaching that school year. Yet I am able to return to the Guilford County classroom the fall of this year of 2008 and officially retire from education. This is a miracle. God is good, and I am appreciative to all.

Acknowledgements

Ancestry.com

Biggs, Kate Townsend; Lumberton, North Carolina library 1989-2007

Carter, Lester Jr. Attorney-retired, Fayetteville, NC

Census; Official Census of Robeson County, 1790

Chapel Hill Press, Chapel Hill, NC

Chowan County Public Library 2007, Records Correspondence

Colton, Norma. York Public Library, Va. Research

Croy, Patricia: Editing Services, Weaverville, NC

Cumberland County Public Libraries 1980-2007

DNA Test, members of TSA correspondence

Documents; land titles, birth records, marriage accounts, Tombstones, wills, etc

Early Virginia Families: Their Broken Roots & Tangled Branches

First Colonist, The; documents of English Settlements, Quinn

Greensboro News and Record, 2006-07

Kilburn, Jayne; Raynham Hall, interview taped 4/1/1980

Landed Barons of Old England, London, published 1886

Macdonald, Flora; Flora MacDonald in America, Her Life and Adventures by Maclean, 1986

Map of North Carolina, S.A. Ashe, Greensboro, 1908.

McLean, Donna. Editing and working with photos, scans, copy

NC Department of Archives and Records, Raleigh, NC

Reunion of 1981 in St Pauls, descendents of William and Ora

Ruffin, Matilda Townsend of Wilson, Miami 1981-84

Ship Lists, York County Library.

St Pauls, NC; Town of St Pauls, a booklet

Thrasher, Jerry   Cumberland County Public Librarian

Townsend, Daniel Earle, of Greenville, SC

Townsend, Daniel Varser

Townsend, Mrs. Daniel (Alma L Sullivan)

Townsend, David Dallum, of Philadelphia; Charlotte

Townsend, James, of Rock Hill, SC and Blowing Rock, NC

Townsend, Lon, of St Pauls

Townsend Society of America, TSA, Oyster Bay, NY

Tyner Townsend, Mrs. John E. "Peggy", Buie, NC 1980-2007

Virginia's 400th Celebration Committee April, 2007 Jamestown

Williamsburg's Virginia: Dr Potts. Theme Pictures

York County Public Library 2006-7, Correspondence

Printed in the United States
133030LV00001B/312/P